JENNY HALLER

JENNY HALLER

DEAN HUGHES

Deseret Book Company
Salt Lake City, Utah

©1983 Deseret Book Company
©1987 Dean Hughes
All rights reserved
Printed in the United States of America

No part of this book may be reproduced in any
form or by any means without permission in writing
from the publisher, Deseret Book Company,
P.O. Box 30178, Salt Lake City, Utah 84130.
Deseret Book is a registered trademark of
Deseret Book Company.

First printing in paperbound edition, September 1987

Library of Congress Cataloging-in-Publication Data

Hughes, Dean, 1943–
    Jenny Haller.

    I. Title.
PS3558.U36J4   1983   813'.54   83-1785
ISBN 0-87747-969-0 (hardbound ed.)
ISBN 0-87579-124-7 (paperbound ed.)

For Delon and Linda Hughes

Chapter 1

Eldon was mad at himself. He had let a couple of pitches get away, and now he was in a tight spot. He walked off the mound and stood for a moment with his hands on his hips, his baseball glove folded in against his side, and stared out at the huge Royals Stadium scoreboard. It was the eighth inning and he had a two-run lead, but there were runners on first and second, and now he had let the count go to two and one. He could hear the barking of the crowd—the restless, nervous sort of noise that people make when they are getting worried.

Stepping back to the pitching rubber, Eldon got his sign from the catcher—fast ball. He checked the runners, slowly, and then fired, really unleashed one. The ball sailed high, but for the moment Eldon didn't notice. Something was wrong with his shoulder. He'd felt something catch and then give way. Now he felt a burning sensation, deep inside his shoulder. He could still move it, however. As he rotated the shoulder, there was nothing he could call pain—just burning.

He stepped forward a little and took the throw from the catcher, then rotated the shoulder again. It was starting to hurt now, but he couldn't worry about it. He needed to concentrate. The batter was digging in, and the crowd was going into that tense, almost silent state that usually came just before a crucial pitch. Potter signaled for a curve ball, and Eldon liked the idea. He could usually get his curve over in a tight situation, and the batter would probably be looking for another fast ball. But even as Eldon brought his arm back, his motion felt unnatural, strained. And when he released the ball, it didn't break at all.

The batter, however, was caught off stride. As the ball floated up almost like a change-up, he took an off-balanced swing and popped it up. Glen Knight took a couple of steps into foul territory, just behind third base, and made the catch. The inning was over, but as Eldon walked back to the dugout, he was worried.

The crowd was going crazy. They obviously didn't understand what had happened. But John Keanon, the manager, looked concerned. "What was that pitch, Hooper?"

Eldon stepped down into the dugout. "It was supposed to be a curve. I didn't get anything on it."

Keanon turned his head and spat into the nearby corner. "You getting tired?"

"I don't know, John. I guess maybe I am."

"Well, we'll let someone else clean up for you in the ninth. You go get a shower and get some ice on that arm. Nice game. I'll tell you, Hooper, you've been carrying us."

As Eldon walked up the tunnel to the team room, he kept moving his shoulder—it was hurting a good deal more now. And he was starting to feel scared.

Eldon Haller had come to the majors right out of high school. Now he was well into his fourth season, and not once had he experienced arm trouble. This would be a particularly terrible time for anything to go wrong. He had been pitching exceptionally well, and the name Eldon Haller—or actually, more often, "Hooper" Haller—was becoming a household word in the country. Part of that might have had to do with the nickname itself, since it called to mind whooping and hollering, and part of it surely came from his good looks and his shy manner, but the attention was still well deserved. Some were saying that he was now the best pitcher in the major leagues.

And so it was understandable that Eldon was frightened when he tried to take off his uniform and found that the movement caused him great pain.

When Eldon got back to his condominium that night, the first thing he did was call Jenny, but no one answered. He had been going with Jenny Davis since his first season in Kansas City. But she had not yet come home this year; she was still in Utah at Brigham Young University, finishing up her last credits for graduation.

Eldon found a cassette and pushed it into his tape player, then made himself a sandwich. He looked around the apartment as he ate. Though it was rather barren looking, with hardly anything on the walls, an elaborate stereo system occupied much of the living room.

Every ten minutes or so he tried Jenny's number. Finally, around one o'clock, she answered.

"Jenny?"

"Yes."

"It's about time you got home; I've been calling you for over an hour."

There was a pause, and then Jenny said, "Is that you, Mom?"

"Very funny. Where have you been?"

"On a date, of course."

Eldon was sorry he'd asked. "Did you go out with that Richard guy again?"

"Mr. Excitement himself."

"You've been seeing a lot of him lately, haven't you?"

4

"Well, don't worry. He's mad at me now. I made him turn on the news so I could hear how your game turned out. He didn't like that. Oh, Eldon, I'm so proud of you. That's seven wins already. You're going to make twenty *easy* this year. Paul James, on the sports news, said you're a shoo-in for the all-star game, and he thinks you're going to get the Cy Young award."

"Were you at his place or something?"

"Whose? Paul James's?"

"No. You know what I mean. Were you at Richard's?"

"Sure. But don't worry. He's completely safe. Mostly he loves my *mind*."

"Well, I don't know." Eldon wasn't sure what to say, but it occurred to him that anyone who could be around Jenny and only notice her mind probably *was* safe. She had pretty gray-blue eyes that were surprisingly light for someone with such dark hair, and she had a smile, with subtle dimples, that always took the starch right out of Eldon. "I just don't like the idea of you spending so much time with him."

"Well, mostly we just study together. But if you really want me to stop going with him, just say so."

"Would you stop if I did?"

"No, but you could still say so."

He knew he should just laugh and let the comment go, but he was in no mood to do so. Instead, he took a breath and let it gust into the telephone, rather obviously.

"Eldon, I was just kidding."

"I know."

"Something's wrong. I know you, Eldon. I can tell that you're upset about something." He didn't answer for a moment. "Am I right?"

"Well, yeah." Eldon was in his bedroom now, sitting on the edge of his bed. The receiver was in his left hand; his right arm lay limp across his lap.

"What is it?"

"I hurt my shoulder tonight."

"Bad?"

"I don't know. I hope not."

"But they said you pitched really well."

"It happened on the second-to-the-last pitch—just before John took me out. It felt like something pulled loose."

"Does the trainer think it's serious?"

"Well, I didn't say too much about it. I told him that I had some pain in my shoulder, but that was all."

"Why, Eldon?"

"I didn't want to make a big deal out of it—have it splashed all over the newspapers. It might not be anything at all. Anyway, we iced it, and that's the only thing we can do for now."

"But you're worried, aren't you."

"A little, I guess." The silence after his words said more than the words themselves.

"Oh, Eldon, I wish I were out there. I saw you on TV last night, and it made me miss you more than ever."

"On TV?"

"It was an interview. On the national news—ABC, I think."

"Oh, yeah. They taped that last week. Did I sound stupid?"

"Come on, Eldon. You never sound stupid. But then, who am I to judge? All I was thinking was, 'Look at the shoulders on that beautiful hunk. What the heck am I doing in Provo when he's in Kansas City?'"

Jenny didn't often say things like that. Eldon was pleased. He knew she was trying to raise his spirits. "When are you coming home?" he asked.

"Just as soon as I can. School is out in about three weeks."

"Jenny, when you get here, we need to talk. I think it's time we get things settled."

"Settled?"

"Yes, and don't sound so scared."

She didn't answer for an uncomfortable number of seconds, and when she did, she sounded too careful. "We really do need to talk," she said at last. It was Eldon who fell silent now, and Jenny must have sensed that she had mishandled the situation. "Eldon, I love you," she said.

"Do you, Jenny?" Eldon's tone was skeptical.

"Come on, Eldon. You know I do."

"I don't know, Jenny. I'm never sure about that." He paused, then added, "Look, this is not a good time for this. We need to talk everything out. I probably shouldn't have even called tonight."

"Eldon, don't worry. Your arm will be okay. And I'll be home soon and we *will* talk then. All right?"

"Sure."

"Eldon, I never worry too much about you. You just seem to know how to make things right. You always seem to know where to find the strength you need."

Eldon thanked Jenny, and by the time he put down the phone his spirits had risen a little. But now he did feel lonely. He wished that Jenny were in town. In the winter he always went back to his home town, Hooper, Utah, and got in a quarter of college at Weber State. That way he wasn't far from her. And by late April she always came back to Kansas City. This was the first time she had stayed in Utah for spring term.

He got up and walked over to the window where he could see the downtown skyline, silhouetted by the city lights. When he stood still like this, his shoulder didn't hurt much. He was starting to believe that nothing was seriously wrong. But then, it had always been easy for him to believe in his own strength—that was something he had never had any reason to doubt. Right now, he was more concerned about Jenny's obvious discomfort with the word *settled*.

He looked out to where the early Mormons had once settled, there in the heart of what was now Kansas City, Missouri. His own great-great-grandfather, Joseph Williams, had lived there as a boy before the Saints had been driven out, and he had always longed to return. But Jackson County wasn't a place of refuge for Eldon. When he went out into the city everyone watched him, crowded around him, asked questions, stuck slips of paper in his face and demanded autographs. It was all very flattering—in some ways he even liked it—but it was so constant. He could never relax and be himself, so he usually fled back to his apartment after a time.

What made the city livable was Jenny, and she wasn't here this year. But having her come home wasn't the whole answer either. He was no longer satisfied with after-game dates and noontime lunches. He wanted her with him all the time. He wanted to be *settled*.

Chapter 2

Within a few days it was obvious to John Keanon and everyone else on the Royals' team that something was wrong with Eldon's arm. Eldon still avoided admitting what he had felt in his shoulder, trying to convince himself that everything would be all right if he took a couple of extra days off. For a time Keanon went along with that, probably hoping it was true, just as Eldon was.

The two were standing in the dugout now, and Eldon was about to walk out to the mound. "Are you all right, Hooper?" Keanon asked, a little doubtfully.

"Yeah, I'm fine, John."

"How did it feel when you were warming up?"

"Well, there was no pain. But I can't seem to cut the ball loose the way I want to. I think I'll have to mix my pitches and just stay away from the hard stuff at first. It's a good warm night. Maybe the arm will loosen up after a couple of innings."

"Well, all right. But listen, Hooper—don't hurt yourself." Keanon spat a dark stream of tobacco juice on the dugout floor, then tucked his hands under his belt, his palms against his big stomach. "If you feel any pain at all, or if it just don't feel right, let's get you out of there. I'm not at all sure you ought to be pitching yet."

"I'll be okay," Eldon said, as he stepped out of the dugout. He hadn't taken two steps before the cheering began. He had become accustomed to that, of course, but now he wondered whether he would let these people down. There was a nervousness in his stomach that he hadn't felt for a long time.

The first inning went rather easily. The Minnesota batters seemed to be expecting his hard stuff, and they were taking awkward swings, feeling for the ball. The second inning went more or less the same way, except that big John Mott, Minnesota's slugger, waited on a pitch and slammed it against the left-field wall. That was the only hit, however, and Eldon got out of the inning again.

But he knew—it was just a matter of time. The shoulder was not loosening up. In the third inning the first batter took an easy swing and poked the ball up the middle for a single. The next batter did almost the same thing. Now two men were on, and the top of the order was coming up.

Eldon knew he had to throw a little harder and to stop serving everything up at the same speed. But when he tried to throw harder, he realized he was reaching for something that wasn't there. The ball was beginning to come up. Fortunately, the next batter swung under the ball and flied out, but he was followed by Sam Folks, who had been on a hot streak for about three weeks.

Potter trotted out to the mound. "Hooper, I don't think we better try that fast ball on him. Is that as hard as you can throw?"

Eldon nodded. He could see the concern in Potter's face. Potter, a big man with huge shoulders, had dark hair that seemed to grow practically down to his eyebrows. He was squinting now, looking almost pained.

"Well, look. Let's try to waste the fast ball outside and see if we can get him out on your slider. But keep it on the inside of the plate, okay?"

Eldon did throw the fast ball outside, and he did keep the slider inside, but the ball didn't move at all. Folks slapped it into right field, and the runner on second scored.

Eldon walked off the mound, turned halfway around, and looked out toward left field. He wanted to go after these guys, but suddenly he felt powerless, frustrated. He took his cap off and wiped his forehead with his sleeve. The night was humid, hot. Maybe he should just tell John he'd better not go any further tonight, but somehow that was more than he was ready to admit.

As he walked back to the pitching rubber, he told himself that maybe he really could throw harder— maybe he was just holding back out of fear. And so he forced the next pitch, really pushed it. The only good thing about it was that the ball sailed too high for the batter to swing.

Potter ran out to the mound. Eldon wouldn't have been surprised to see John coming out too, but he was standing on the dugout steps, clapping his hands, yelling encouragement. Potter handed Eldon the ball. "Hooper, are you okay? Is that shoulder hurting?"

"No, but I can't get much on the ball."

Potter fidgeted, stepping from one foot to the other, hitting his mask against his leg. Eldon missed Frank Heaton, who had been traded for Potter during the winter. Heaton had always been calm, and he could always help Eldon relax. "Well, listen, Hooper. Woodall is a good hitter, but he's not all that fast. We got a good chance of doubling him if we can get a ground ball. So let's keep the ball down—and away from him. Don't try to throw too hard. Don't try to use what you don't have."

Eldon nodded, but he was a little irritated. Potter made it sound worse than it was. Eldon wasn't just a hard thrower; he was also smart. He could finesse a batter when he wanted to. He was going to get Woodall right now.

He started out with a slider at the knees. Though Woodall didn't swing, the umpire called it a strike. The crowd responded, almost with relief; but then the noise subsided quickly as the people seemed to sense that something was wrong.

Eldon was concentrating on Potter's glove, now outside and low. He went with the fast ball, keeping it a little outside the strike zone, but Woodall didn't chase it. Then he went back to the slider, almost in the same place, and Woodall let it go again. The count moved to two and one.

Eldon got the sign—back to the fast ball, inside corner and low. He straightened, took a deep breath, checked the runners, then threw as hard as he could. It wasn't a bad pitch, though it was up just a little, but it didn't have Eldon's usual speed. Woodall hit it hard.

Eldon turned and watched as the ball sailed high and long, then dropped beyond the left-field fence, hitting the little turf-covered incline. It seemed to stick there for a moment, and then it rolled down, disappearing behind the fence. Eldon sensed the runners rounding the bases, but he kept looking out to where the ball had gone. He felt empty.

John was coming now. Eldon could hear him tromping across the synthetic turf. The stadium was almost silent—as quiet as Eldon had ever known it.

"Well, Hooper, I guess I did the wrong thing tonight. I should've held you out for a while yet."

Eldon turned around. "John, I'm not sure a couple of days would've made any difference. There's something really wrong."

"Well, now, don't get too fussed up about it. Every guy who ever threw a baseball got a sore arm sooner or later. This thing might clear up faster than you think."

Eldon didn't like what he saw on John's face. There didn't seem to be much conviction behind his words. The relief pitcher was getting out of the car now. As he approached, Keanon said to Eldon, "You'll be okay. But it might take some patience."

Eldon nodded, then walked off the mound. Suddenly the crowd stood up, the motion so startling that Eldon almost stopped. There was no cheering; rather, people were applauding. This was something new—a level of admiration Eldon had never experienced before. As he passed through the dugout the players lined up to shake his hand. They were saying not to worry, that it was all right. Eldon understood, and he appreciated what they were doing. But it all seemed too much like a retirement party.

Chapter 3

Jenny spent the evening at the BYU library. She had a big test coming up the next morning, but the whole time she wondered what was happening at the game in Kansas City. When Eldon had called and said he was going to pitch, he had seemed rather nervous about it. This worried Jenny. She could be feisty, sometimes even rebellious, and Eldon always seemed mild-mannered by comparison. But the truth was, Eldon had much more genuine confidence. And Jenny knew it.

Jenny also had other things on her mind. She knew the time was coming soon when Eldon would want her to make a decision about their future, and she hadn't yet told him about some of the things she now was considering. But for now she didn't want to think about it anymore. Finally, at about nine-thirty, she tossed her things in her book bag and headed down the stairs.

As she reached the main floor, she saw Dr. Keith, the professor who was giving the test the next day. "Hi, Brother Keith," she said, and she probably would have kept going, but he stopped.

"Well, hello, Jenny. How are you doing?"

"Not very well. I'm not ready for your test tomorrow."

"I don't believe that for a minute," he said, carefully enunciating his words. He was older, nearly retirement age, and had a wonderful intensity about him when he lectured. He had a way of seeking eye contact and then holding it as he spoke. Sometimes Jenny felt that he was giving the whole lecture just to her.

"No, it's true," Jenny said. "I'm going to get up really early in the morning and hit the books some more."

"Well, now, that's not such a bad thing."

"You don't know how much I hate to get up early in the morning."

He chuckled. "No more than I do," he said.

Jenny felt self-conscious. She loved to listen to Dr. Keith lecture, but outside class she never knew what to say to him. And yet he seemed to go out of his way to chat with her.

"Jenny, what have you decided about next year? Are you going on to graduate school?"

"I'm not sure what I'm going to do." The decision again. "I took the law exams last winter and got pretty good scores. So just for the heck of it I applied to law school here at BYU. And I got accepted."

"That's good, Jenny—although I'd rather have you in our English program. I suspect you received *very* good scores on the exams."

"Well, there were some other people who did better."

"Not much, I'm sure." That was true, but Jenny didn't say so. "And what if you don't go to law school?"

"I'll probably go home to Kansas City."

"And?"

"Get married."

"To the baseball player?"

"Yes."

"I thought you were dating another fellow now— the one I saw you with at the play the other night."

"Well, I have dated him some."

"Wouldn't he be better for you, Jenny? I mean, he . . . well, I suppose that's none of my business."

"No, go ahead. What were you going to say?"

"It's just that you and he seem to have so much in common. I have a hard time picturing you married to a professional athlete."

"Why?"

"Well, I don't know. I guess I have my stereotype for the athletic sorts. Maybe that's not fair. But is he worthy of you, Jenny?"

Jenny laughed. "Worthy of *me*? I think most people would ask the question the other way around."

Dr. Keith slipped his hands into his trouser pockets. He looked at her seriously, the wrinkles around his eyes tightening. "You know, Jenny, the charming thing about you is that you don't know what a marvelous person you are. You're very pretty, and you're pleasant. There are lots of pretty young women around, but very, very few are so sharp—so quick. You have a fine mind, Jenny, and I have the feeling you are just beginning to tap your capabilities."

"Well, I . . ." Jenny didn't feel very quick right now. She couldn't think of anything to say.

"Does your baseball player friend have any brains?"

"Yes, he does, Brother Keith. He hasn't had time to get much college behind him yet, but he's really smart."

"Of course. He might be smart—but can he really think? Can he keep up with you? Or will he always feel inferior?"

"No, he doesn't feel inferior." The thought was amusing to Jenny. "And there's no reason he should. He reads constantly. He's really more devoted to learning than I am."

"Well, that's good. But Jenny, make sure he'll be fair to you. It won't be right if he makes you waste your mind. You're a gifted young woman; he has no right to take that from you." Jenny didn't want to make some stupid little denial that would come out sounding like false humility, but she was amazed. She knew she had done well in school, but she had certainly never thought of herself as gifted.

"What's the hurry anyway, Jenny? You're only—what?—twenty-one? twenty-two?"

"I just turned twenty-two."

"And the baseball player? How old is he?"

"He'll be twenty-one this summer."

"Well, then, I don't see the hurry."

Jenny looked down for a moment. Actually, she didn't see the hurry either. Slowly she said, "Well, he's been playing since he got out of high school—and he's alone all the time. He's really tired of that."

"Yes, I can understand that. It's much easier to say there's no hurry when a fellow is my age." Dr. Keith chuckled. "Forgive me for meddling," he went on, "but I do find myself feeling rather paternal about my best students."

"I appreciate that, Brother Keith."

"Jenny, if you don't put your mind to good use, you'll have wasted God's gift to you. I just hope your young man is one who understands that."

Jenny nodded and stepped back just a little. As much as she liked hearing these words, she was embarrassed. "I don't think that's a problem," she finally said.

"Well, good. But, Jenny, there are things you should be doing with your life. I don't know what they are—and I don't suppose you do either. But I suspect you ought to find out before you spend your life sitting on the bench while your husband is the only one playing the game."

"He's really a fair person, Brother Keith. I don't think you need to worry about that. The only thing that bothers me is that he's so . . . well, so famous. It kind of scares me that I might get sort of lost."

"I think that *is* a danger, Jenny." He pushed his hands down into his pockets. "But I get the distinct impression you're in love with him. That's an awfully good sign." He winked, then smiled. "I've seen the boy on TV. He looks as though he just flew in from Mount Olympus. What a fine-looking young man. You'll be a stunning couple."

Jenny felt herself blushing. "Well, thanks," she said, taking another step away.

"Come and see me if you like. I have lots more I could say. We old men have wisdom, you know; we come equipped with it. But then, I suspect right now you need your answers from a higher source."

"It might not hurt to go through channels," she said. "I sometimes have trouble getting through."

Dr. Keith nodded and said that he knew the problem; then he said good night, and Jenny pushed through the library doors. Outside she drew a deep breath. Though it was cool and a layer of clouds obscured the stars, crickets were chirping; it was finally beginning to feel like summer.

Jenny wished she were home. She had never been away during the summer before. For the past three years summer had meant dates with Eldon and delicious full days with him on her days off from work. Somehow she had managed to think of her life that way: three seasons for school followed by one at home with Eldon.

Eldon had always talked of marrying when she finished college, and she had looked forward to that too. But lately she'd begun thinking that she might not feel ready that soon. She knew that many young women who graduated unmarried became worried that they had lost their chance, but for some reason, she didn't feel that way. Maybe knowing that Eldon was there, waiting for her, had given her a sense of security. Yet she also knew that Eldon wasn't going to wait forever.

Jenny really did want to marry Eldon, but Dr.

Keith's words kept coming back to her now as she walked along through the campus. Was she really gifted? The thought seemed rather corny. And yet, for some time she had felt that she wanted to do something with her life—something important and meaningful. "It won't be right if he makes you waste your mind," she repeated to herself.

Chapter 4

Eldon spent some time getting his shoulder and arm packed with ice and discussing the situation with Cy, the trainer. By the time the other players came back to the clubhouse, he was dressed and ready to leave. The players would have to let him go without bothering him, but Cy told him to stick around, that John wanted to talk to him.

Eldon walked over and sat down on a chair near Keanon's office. Most of the players were changing or had already hit the showers. They were subdued, not saying much. They had just taken a real pounding, and their depression was deepened by the knowledge that their best pitcher was having arm troubles.

Clyde Becker, the Royals' utility infielder, was standing at the end of the room, his shirt off. He pulled off his shoes and then looked over at Eldon.

"Hey, Hooper," he yelled, "how come you're sitting by the manager's door? Have you been a bad boy?"

Most of the players turned around and looked at Eldon. "You must not have seen the game, Becker," Eldon said. "I've been *very, very* bad." Eldon had meant simply to return Becker's banter, but he had sounded entirely too serious.

That didn't bother Becker, though. "No, no, Hooper—you just don't understand what you've got now. You have the only natural change-up fast ball in the league. You just need to learn how to use it." He got up from his stool and assumed a pitcher's stance, staring in to get the sign. "Okay, Hooper, watch this and you'll see how it's done." Everyone was watching by now, even the reporters in the room. Becker stroked his mustache a couple of times and then fidgeted around, all the while steadily watching the imaginary catcher at the other end of the room. Then, in ultra-slow motion, he went through a wind-up and delivery. He brought the ball through and, still in slow motion, pretended to stumble forward. Then he righted himself and started to trot toward the other end of the room.

"Okay, Hooper, now watch. Here's your pitch coming toward home plate. It's moving so slow that it's hard to see. All right, I've moved ahead of it now." He jogged on ahead and then spun around and crouched into a catcher's position. "Okay, here it comes. The batter swings and misses—way out ahead of it. But he swings again—a vicious cut. He's still out in front of it. He takes one more cut and misses again, as the ball suddenly dies for want of speed." Becker pretended to catch the ball, again in slow motion, but then he jumped up, stepped back, and in a booming voice yelled, "That's three strikes. You're out of there!" He made a wild motion with his right hand, almost falling backwards.

No one really thought it was as funny as Becker did, but at least the tension was broken a little. Eldon had the good sense to get up and say, "Now, how was it?" He started the slow-motion wind-up.

Becker began walking toward him. "It's the same fast ball you were throwing tonight—except with maybe just a little more muscle behind it."

Eldon stopped his motion and started to laugh. He

was searching for something to come back with when Keanon's door opened. Keanon glanced around quickly. "I'm glad to see all you guys enjoying yourselves," he said. "I guess it's easy to lose once you get used to it."

"Oh, no, John, not at all," Becker said. "But if you'd let me play more, I think we could gradually get the hang of it."

Keanon didn't laugh, but he didn't explode either. Becker was the only guy on the team who could get away with something like that.

"Show him your new pitch, Hooper," Becker said, as the door shut behind Eldon and Keanon.

"Is Becker bugging you?" Keanon asked.

"No. He was just joking around."

"As usual." Keanon had not yet changed out of his uniform, but he had his shoes off, which made him look shorter than ever. He tucked his fingers under his belt and nodded toward Cy, who was sitting by the door. "Me and Cy have been talking about your shoulder. We're thinking we better fly you out to Los Angeles to see a doctor. There's a guy out there who specializes in athletic injuries. He's the one who worked on Buttars. We thought it might not hurt to have him take a look at you."

Eldon wasn't sure what this meant. Maybe Cy was worried. "Okay," he said. "When?"

"Right away. We'll have to make arrangements. I think we might as well get you on a plane tomorrow. Maybe this doc could see you the day after that, if he's not out of town or something."

"All right. Will the front office make the arrangements, or should I—"

"Yeah. I'll have them give you a call tomorrow, once they've got things worked out. I don't know how long you'll have to be out there, but you wouldn't be pitching for a while anyway now."

Eldon knew that was true, but he hated the sound

of it. He liked to get right back out there as soon as he could after a loss. "If the doctor thinks it's coming along all right, when do you think you might use me again?"

"I just don't know, Hooper. We'll have to keep watching this thing. I don't think there's any question that we rushed you tonight."

Eldon nodded, watching Keanon. The man looked troubled. "It didn't hurt much, John. I just couldn't loosen up enough to really let the ball pop."

"Listen, Eldon," Keanon said, "you were the youngest kid ever to come up to the majors with our organization. You've been throwing the ball hard for three years—and you threw hard in high school. An arm can only take so much." He walked over and sat on the front edge of his desk. "Who knows? Maybe you're not going to have quite the fast ball you've always had. But you're not just a power pitcher—you know how to pitch to spots and how to change speeds."

"It sounds like you think something's seriously wrong."

"No, no. I'm not saying that. Maybe it's just a little muscle pull. But I don't want you to get too discouraged if the doctor thinks it *is* something serious."

Eldon nodded. He didn't like John's tone at all. It sounded as though Cy had already made his own diagnosis and had told John that things didn't look good. "Well, anyway, I'll see what the doctor has to say. I hope I won't have to be out there too long."

"So do I," Keanon said. "No one wants you back in the rotation more than I do."

And so Eldon left. The players were clearing out now; no one said anything to Eldon except Les Huntley, who stopped him and asked him whether he wanted to go out for something to eat. Les was a rookie, the same age as Eldon, and the two of them had been put together as roommates on road trips. Les had been taking the usual ribbing from the older players, and he had gotten off to a slow start at the plate. It was not an easy time for him, and he tended to look to Eldon for support.

"I don't think so tonight," Eldon said. "I'm pretty beat."

"Yeah, well, I can understand that. But I thought you might not want to just go back to your place after . . . you know . . . after what happened."

Eldon laughed a little. "Actually, *nothing* happened. This is the kind of night you just have to forget."

"I wish I could do that," Les said. He shook his head and looked down. He was a big man with a powerful, stocky frame, and yet there was something childlike in his face: the dark hair that drooped down on his forehead and the quick way he had of glancing at people and then avoiding further eye contact. "Night before last—after I struck out when John put me in to pinch-hit—I couldn't go to sleep for hours."

"Everybody's put in a few nights like that, Les. But it gets easier after you've been up here for a while."

"I hope so. I hope I *stay* long enough to find out."

"Well, we all hope that, Les. The last couple of days I've been wondering what might happen to me now."

"You don't think it's too serious, do you?"

"I don't know. No, I guess not." Eldon pushed the hair back from his own forehead. His hair had a tendency to fall forward much the way Les's did, though Eldon's was blond and sunbleached, almost white in the front. "But I'll tell you something, Les. I've been thinking about what I would do if I couldn't keep playing baseball. And that kind of scares me."

"I know. That's what I was thinking about in bed the other night."

They walked out of the clubhouse together, took the elevator upstairs, and then walked out to their cars. Neither said much more. They both seemed lost in their thoughts.

The traffic on the freeway was still fairly heavy, but

Eldon didn't care. He was in no real hurry to get home, in spite of what he'd told Les. When he arrived, he put a record on his stereo and lay down on his bed with his clothes on. His shoulder was beginning to ache again, but he didn't think much about that. He had too many other things to consider.

After about ten minutes, he sat up and called Jenny. He told her that he was going to the West Coast and that he was thinking he'd like to stop by and see her before he returned to Kansas City. Jenny seemed very happy about that, but when Eldon said it would be a good chance for them to talk, she seemed to get rather nervous again. Something was going on that Eldon didn't understand, and it didn't help things right now.

But Eldon let it go. He told her he wasn't sure when he would get there, but that he would call from Los Angeles. He also told her not to tell anyone he was coming; he wasn't sure he'd have time to go see his parents, and he didn't want someone from the press to find out he was there and write about it or put it on the television news. His parents might not understand. It was strange to have to worry about such things, but the press had become so much a part of Eldon's life that he had learned to calculate for it in everything he did.

"Are you feeling all right?" Jenny asked.

"Sure."

"But you feel bad about the game, don't you."

"Well, not that much. I just shouldn't have pitched yet."

"Eldon, you say that, but I know you. You're really hurting tonight."

Eldon didn't say much. He didn't want to sound like some rookie kid. And he didn't want to say he was scared. But all the same, he was glad she understood.

Chapter 5

Five days later, on Monday evening, Eldon arrived in Provo. He drove straight to Jenny's apartment, where he found a note on the door explaining where to find her in the library. He was disappointed, but then, he had not been able to give her an exact time when he would get out of Los Angeles.

He left the car at her place and walked the three blocks to the university. It was a nice night, mild, even a little cool. He felt the peace hovering under the trees as he climbed the hill to the upper campus. But he was nervous. He still wasn't sure what to expect from Jenny.

Eldon found her sitting at a table. Two other girls were at the opposite end. He stopped and, for a moment, just looked at her. She was wearing a simple T-shirt, light blue, and her dark hair was down, resting on her shoulders. As he stepped closer to the table, she looked up. Her eyes remained calm, but she smiled, her dimples appearing. "Excuse me, young lady," Eldon said. "I'm trying to find a book, but I seem to be having trouble with the Dewey Decimal System. Do you think you could help me?"

"I'll do my very best," she said, and she slid her chair back and stood up.

Eldon glanced at the other girls at the table, and they were both looking at him curiously, as though they wondered if he were serious. "I think it should be down this way," he said, leading the way down an aisle. He soon turned into the stacks, walked halfway down a row, and turned around. Jenny kept right on walking—into his arms. Eldon said, "That book has to be around here somewhere," but he continued to hold her close.

"I'm looking for it," Jenny murmured, her face against his chest and her eyes closed. Eldon kissed her hair, then moved back just a little to see her face. "I'm glad you finally got here," she said. "I've been telling myself that I have to study, but I haven't gotten much done."

"Do you have to study some more tonight?"

"Yes, but I'm not going to."

Eldon kissed her and then he held her close again, and they stood that way, between the shelves of books, for some time. This was the first time Eldon had felt really good since the night he had hurt his shoulder. "Let's go, okay?" he said finally.

Jenny went ahead this time. She walked back to the table and got her books, and then, just before she turned to walk away with Eldon, she said, "Who would have thought this could happen so quickly? But I knew I loved you the moment I looked at you." She said this with amazing seriousness.

Eldon couldn't help grinning. He looked over at the two girls. They were staring.

Jenny took Eldon's arm then, and they walked off into the golden sunset—or so the girls must have thought. Actually, Eldon was saying, "Jenny, you're really out of your mind, you know that?"

As they came out of the library and into the cool air, Eldon was reminded that he wanted to have a serious talk with Jenny. He needed to control the mood.

"Jenny," he said, "I left the car over at your place. I thought it would be nice just to walk."

"Good. I feel like walking."

"Would you like to go someplace—maybe get something to eat?"

"Okay. I didn't get time before."

"Is there a good place around here?"

"Let's just go to the Wilkinson Center. You can blow some big money and buy me an ice cream cone."

"Don't you want something more than that?"

"Well, all right. I'll have a *good* meal. I'll have a banana split."

Suddenly Eldon stopped. "Jenny, are there many people over there?"

"Oh, that's right. You're trying to stay out of sight. Do people out here recognize you that much?"

"Well, you know. Some do." He thought about it for a moment. "Well, never mind. Let's go over there. Probably no one will pay any attention."

At the snack bar there were plenty of people around, but no one seemed to notice Eldon. Jenny ordered a banana split; Eldon said he had eaten on the plane and only wanted something to drink. "What's this stuff?" he asked, pointing to one of the soft drinks set on ice.

Jenny turned and looked. "Oh, that's a no-caffeine cola. You ought to try it."

So Eldon got one, with a glass of ice. While he was paying at the cash register, Jenny walked ahead. She found a table far away from most of the people, even away from most of the light. Eldon followed and sat down across from her.

"Okay, now tell me what the doctor said."

He had popped the lid on the can and was pouring his drink into the glass. "Well, not much more than I told you on the phone. The rotator cuff is definitely torn. It's the same injury that knocked Jeff Buttars out of baseball, but mine isn't nearly so bad. He thinks it will heal if I'm careful. He's starting me on an exercise program."

"How do you feel about that?"

"I guess it's better than if he'd said he wanted to start cutting. I'd miss the whole season that way." He took a rather large gulp of his drink, then put the glass down quickly and grimaced. "That stuff's awful! It tastes like syrup."

"I know." She was too busy eating to look up. "I just wanted you to *experience* it."

Eldon shook his head in mock disgust. "No caffeine, maybe, but enough sugar to make you sick."

Jenny paused, then smiled. "Sounds like a description of BYU," she said. All the same, she went back to her ice cream, seeming to tolerate the sweetness of chocolate sauce quite well. Eldon kept watching her, waiting for her to look at him again.

"So how long before you pitch again?"

"I don't know. At least a couple of weeks. And then just a few innings."

Jenny looked up then, studying Eldon, and her look became gradually more serious. "Eldon, have you thought about what you would do if you couldn't pitch any more?"

"I don't think there's any danger of that, Jenny. I'll just work as hard as I have to. I'll be okay."

"But what if—"

"Hi, Eldon. I *thought* that was you sitting over here."

Eldon looked up; a girl was standing by the table. She seemed familiar to him, yet he couldn't think who she was. "Oh, hi," he said.

"What are you doing here in the middle of baseball season?"

"Well, I had to see a doctor in California. I hurt my—"

"Oh, that's right. I heard about that. Well, at least it gives you a chance to stop by and see old Hooper."

He remembered. She was from his home town—one of the Cottle girls. Could she be old enough for BYU? "Well, I may not get time to get up there."

"Oh, I get it. You're just sneaking in a little visit with your girl friend." She looked at Jenny.

"Not exactly. I—"

"I'm Linda Cottle," the girl was saying to Jenny. "I've known Eldon since I was in grade school and he was in junior high. I had this really *huge* crush on him." She shook her curly hair and gave a quick little smile.

"Excuse me, Linda, this is Jenny Davis. She's from Kansas City."

"You lucky duck," Linda said. "If you can hook old Eldon, you've really done all right."

Lucky duck? Eldon couldn't believe this. But Jenny was laughing. She glanced at Eldon.

"So you're at BYU now, huh?" Eldon said, trying hard to think of something to change the subject.

"Right," Linda said, stretching the word into several syllables. "And I just *love* it. It's really a special place. I finished up my high-school credits before my senior year was over, so I decided to come down here for spring term. It's the best decision I ever made. I've met so many really special people here."

"Well, that's great." There was a pause. She was still standing there, still smiling. Eldon didn't know what to do with her. "So what are you going to major in?" This seemed to strike Jenny as amusing. She ducked her head and put her hand to her forehead.

"Well, I don't know, Eldon. I don't think it really matters too much. You know—maybe I won't last that long around here." She winked and then sort of shrugged, all the while glowing with smiles. "I'm writing to two different missionaries who'll both be home next spring, so—who knows?" She giggled at herself. "I mainly want the experience of being here for a while. There's really a choice spirit at the Y. I had heard about it, but I didn't know how special it was till I came down here."

Eldon nodded. "I'm sure that's true," he said, trying to be very serious, but aware that Jenny was still ducking her head to hide her reaction.

"Well, anyway, it was good to see you, Eldon. Say, I've been wanting to ask you, why do they call you 'Hooper' instead of 'Hooper'?" The first time she pronounced the word so that it rhymed with Cooper, but the second time she said it the way people from the town did, the double "o" sounding like the "o's" in "good."

"I don't know. That's just the way some of the guys on the team pronounced it, and they started calling me that. Now everyone does."

"Oh, well, I guess it doesn't matter. At least you put us on the map. Anyway, I gotta go. It looks like my family-home-evening group is getting ready to take off." She started away, then turned back. "Nice to meet you, Jenny. I hope you catch old Eldon. He's really a special guy."

"That he is," Jenny said. "I often say so myself."

"See ya. I'll tell your folks I saw you next time I get home for a weekend."

Eldon thought about stopping her and telling her not to do that, but he couldn't bring himself to do it. "I guess I'll have to call my parents," he said to Jenny.

"Might be a good idea." She was smiling again. "That Linda is really a *special* girl. But then, BYU probably made her that way. We get *special* education here."

"She's only seventeen," Eldon said.

"I know. But if I hear that *word* around here one more time, I think I'll gag."

"What, *special*?"

Jenny grabbed her throat and pretended to be

choking, but Eldon wished she'd just let the whole thing go. He wanted to move the talk back to something serious. "Should we get out of here?" he said.

"Just a second. I have to finish my dinner."

After a few more spoonfuls, she pushed the dish back, and they got up to leave. Suddenly a couple of guys stopped them. "Aren't you Eldon Haller?" The speaker was tall and well dressed. Something about his manner made Eldon think he was probably a newly returned missionary.

Jenny walked on a few steps, then turned and waited. "Yes," Eldon said, taking another step, trying to get away quickly.

"See, I told you," said the young man to his friend. "What are you doing out here, Eldon?"

A whole series of questions followed. Eldon kept his answers brief and tried to follow Jenny, who was edging away from him. Finally, when the shorter one asked what sort of guy Glen Knight really was, Eldon said, "Oh, about like you'd expect. Look, you guys, I have to run. It was nice talking to you." Some other students had gathered around and were listening to the conversation. Others in the room were looking over, the word apparently having gotten around the place that Hooper Haller was there.

"Hey, right," the tall one said. "Good luck with your shoulder. I'm just *sure* it will be all right."

"Thanks," Eldon said, hurrying to catch up to Jenny, who was nearly to the door by now.

When they got outside, she said, "I can't believe how those guys were talking to you. It was like you were some higher form of life. It's getting worse all the time. Is your whole life like that now?"

Eldon stopped her and turned her toward him. "No, Jenny. Only half of it. The rest of the time I'm by myself in my apartment or in some hotel room. It's not fun, Jenny. It's lonely—and most of the time it doesn't seem to mean very much."

"I know," Jenny said. "I've been lonely too. I've missed being with you this summer."

Eldon took her in his arms and held her for a long time. He wished that he could just go back to Kansas City now—and take her with him.

Chapter 6

Eldon and Jenny walked over to the side of the library and sat down on a little retaining wall. He put his arm around her shoulders. The campus looked pretty under the night lighting, with the well-kept lawns and the pretty flower gardens.

"I'll tell you something," Jenny said, "but you have to promise not to tell anyone I said it."

"All right."

"I love this place. I joke about it all the time—and some things really drive me crazy. Like some of the self-righteous students. But I really have the feeling that these four years have *re*-created me."

"In what sense?"

"I just think I'm a different person. Or maybe I'm just finally becoming one. I've actually gotten to the point where I like to learn."

"Well, I envy you that, Jenny. That's one thing I've missed out on for the most part."

"Listen, I'm just trying to catch up with you. I doubt I'll ever have the self-control to read as much as you do, without anyone to force me to do it. I need the structure a college gives me." Eldon didn't say anything. He had the feeling she was leading up to something, and he felt a little uncomfortable about it.

"That's what drives me nuts about someone like your friend Linda. She comes down here to get herself a husband, and the education means absolutely nothing to her."

"Getting a husband isn't such a bad thing, is it?"

She gave Eldon a little push in the ribs with her elbow. "I don't know. I never *got* one."

"Maybe it's about time you did."

Eldon felt Jenny tense just a little, and he wasn't sure why. She stood up, saying, "Eldon, after such a nice meal I need some dessert. Let's go get something."

"Jenny, we need to talk. The whole reason I came out here was to—"

"I know, I know. But let's walk back to my place now. Maybe we can drive over to the grocery store and find something good to eat. Come on." She grabbed his hand and pulled. "We have plenty of time."

Eldon knew that Jenny was retreating, but he let her get away with it. They drove to a store and bought some frozen pizza "for dessert," then took it back to her apartment and sat at the kitchen table while they waited for the oven to heat up.

Jenny talked about her classes and asked about her friends in the ward back in Missouri where her father was bishop. As they talked, Eldon had the feeling she was edging away from anything really important.

Long after the oven was heated up, Jenny got up and put the pizza in. "Eldon, you never did tell me what you would do if you had to quit playing baseball."

"I don't know how you can say that so casually, Jenny. That's my whole career you're talking about."

"Well, I didn't mean to sound that way. But you must be thinking about it."

"Yeah, I'm thinking about it—but I'm trying not to."

"Don't you think you should?"

"No, I don't. Right now the only thing I want to do is get myself ready to pitch again. If something happened—maybe my shoulder got torn again, or something like that—then I'd just have to face it, but it seems negative to me to stew about it right now."

"Okay, I can see that. But let me ask the question another way. What are you going to do when you quit playing baseball, no matter when that is?"

"I don't know." Eldon looked down at the grain in the little pine table and thought for a time. "I hardly know how to think about that right now. It's ten or fifteen years off, I hope—maybe more than that. Right now I just don't want to have anything go wrong and take my career away from me. I want to stop when I *choose* to stop."

"When will that be?"

"I don't know. I'm making a lot of money now, but that's not really the most important thing to me. I want—"

"How much, Eldon? The paper said your new contract is for two million dollars. Is that true?"

He looked over in her direction, but not really at her. "It amounts to that. A lot of it is in deferred payments and investments. It takes about twenty lawyers just to figure out the contract."

"Two million for how many years?"

"Four."

"What if you *did* get hurt? Would you still get the money?"

"Yes."

"Why is it you never talk about money, Eldon?"

"I don't know. I guess it's sort of embarrassing. I'm not sure anybody ought to get that much money—especially for playing a game."

"You know, Eldon, you could just invest that two million and live well forever. You wouldn't have to *do* anything."

"I know."

"Doesn't that make you feel strange—like there's really nothing else left to do?"

"No, not at all. After baseball I can do something I enjoy, whether it pays well or not. But that's not really the issue. There are certain things I want to accomplish in baseball, and they don't have anything to do with how much I get paid."

"What kind of things?"

"Well, it's nothing specific. I'm not trying to break any particular record or anything like that. But I've been throwing a baseball since I was a little kid. Before I quit, I'd like to throw the thing as well as I can—maybe even as well as it *can* be thrown. Can you understand that? I know baseball's just a game, but—"

"No, don't say that. I understand exactly what you're saying. I really do. But see, that's the problem. I want something like that in *my* life. I want to be really good at something."

"That's good, Jenny," Eldon said, but he was watching her carefully. He wasn't sure what she was trying to say. She looked back at him for just a moment, then got up and opened the oven door to check the pizza. When she turned back around, she remained standing as she said, "Eldon, I've been accepted to law school here at BYU. I'm thinking about going this fall."

Eldon sat still for quite some time, watching her. He could see what it meant, and he felt something inside him begin to sink. "Why didn't you tell me?" he finally said.

She shrugged, actually looking rather frail in her T-shirt, her shoulders appearing so slight. But Eldon knew better. She was anything but frail. She was strong and independent. "I didn't tell you because I wasn't sure what I was going to do."

"Jenny, you just said more than you realize."

"What do you mean?"

"It should have been something we talked about, together."

"But it's *my* decision."

"Not totally, Jenny. It's something we could have worked out. You could come out to Kansas City and go to law school there. We could get married and—"

"And I'd start having babies, Eldon. And I'd never get *my* chance to accomplish something." She slid her fingers into the pockets of her jeans. "See, that's the problem. I'm jealous of you. You're good at something. You're famous. You're *somebody*. I'm still searching around. But I want to know that there's something *I* can do, so that I can have some pride in myself. I don't want just to be Jenny Haller, Eldon's wife. I want some identity of my own. I could just share your goals and spend your money, and sort of blend into you—and I guess that's what most people would say I *should* do—but it scares me, Eldon. I feel like I'm losing all my sense of self."

"Don't you want to have a family?"

"Of course I do. But that's the trouble. I want everything. I want *you*, but I don't want to lose *me* in the process. I want to be married, but I also want law school. And I don't want to have to choose between the things I want. So I guess I've been stalling, and that's why I haven't said anything."

Eldon didn't respond. He felt everything slipping away from him. This was not at all what he had hoped for in coming to see Jenny.

Jenny came back to the table and sat down. She reached out and put her hand on his arm. "Eldon, we're still not that old. Would it make that much difference if we waited a while before we got married?"

Eldon's pride was stung. He was not going to beg her. What he really wanted to do was just leave and not have to show that he was hurt. "It would make a difference to me," he said. "I'm tired of my situation—

being alone." He slid his chair back, distancing himself from Jenny's reach. "The truth is, Jenny, I'm not sure that you really want to marry me at all. I've never been sure of that."

"That's because I'm more selfish than you, Eldon. I always hold something back. It's frightening to me to commit myself."

He nodded, sat for a few seconds, and then stood up. "Listen," he said, "I think maybe I better drive up to Hooper. I ought to spend a little time with my parents while I have a chance."

"Eldon, don't go. Not yet. Can't we talk about this?"

This angered Eldon just enough to bring back the strength to his voice. "Jenny, you know as well as I do that you are going to make your own decision. I can listen, if that's what you want, but if I try to talk you into anything, it just won't work."

Jenny looked down, away from his eyes, and tears began to slide down her cheeks. She reached up and wiped them away with the back of her hand. "I *do* love you," she said.

"You need to think this over, Jenny. Maybe when you come home, we can have another look at things."

"Okay. But don't leave yet. Stay with me awhile."

He was glad she wanted him there, and he was touched by the sincerity of her emotion, but he wanted to leave. He wanted to run from the disappointment that the whole situation represented. It was just too much, with so many other worries already on his mind. All the same, he stayed. They ate very little of the pizza, and they didn't even talk much, at least about anything that mattered.

Before he left he did take her in his arms, but not for long. He was having trouble with his emotions. He wanted to demand that she marry him, that she forget about law school—or he wanted to get mad, or even plead with her. Anything would be better than just to leave things as they were. But he was not going to make a fool of himself. He stepped out on the porch, stopped, and turned around. "Personally," he said, "I like the name Jenny Haller."

She smiled. "It sounds like some dumb little town in Montana or Wyoming."

Eldon laughed as Jenny came out and kissed him again. And then he left. He arrived in Hooper after his parents had already gone to bed, but they were happy to see him, and at least he got a chance to sleep in his "own" bed that night. It was better than being back in his condo in Kansas City. All the same, he wished that he had a game to pitch in a day or two. Life always seemed to have more focus, more meaning, when he had a game coming up.

Chapter 7

Jenny went to bed right after Eldon left. Sleep was always her easiest escape. But she woke up early the next morning, as the sun began filling the room. She could hear sparrows outside chattering and flitting about. It was a peaceful time of the day, and she lay there for quite some time before she got up. She wondered what Eldon was doing, how he was feeling. She even thought of calling him at his parents' house, but she didn't do it. She also avoided thinking about law school or marriage—or anything about her future. She just lay there, feeling alone and a little scared. She had no idea what she was going to do, and she wasn't sure she could find out. Over and over she had prayed about all these problems, but nothing seemed to be coming clear to her.

She got up earlier than usual and studied for a while. Or at least she looked at words on pages. She soon gave that up and made herself some toast. The cold pizza was still on the table. She took a bite, but aging hadn't improved it. She dumped the whole thing in the garbage.

As she ate the toast with a glass of milk, she sat at the little table where she'd sat with Eldon the night before. The situation struck her as sort of ironic. Why should she be alone like this, in this dumb little apartment? All she had to do was go home to Kansas City. She could have a home; Eldon could afford to build anything he liked—or anything *she* liked. She could wake up to him instead of this emptiness, and she could spend long mornings with him before he had to go off to the baseball park. Eldon was so good to be with, so unaffected and pleasant. The thought of being held by him, of having her head against his shoulder, of feeling his firmness and confidence—it was all so inviting this morning. Maybe the decision should be as simple as that; it really did feel right when she perceived it in visual and tactile terms, keeping her head out of it all.

But she couldn't shut off the other emotions. She feared that she might put her head against his shoulder and never lift it up again—that she might get lost in him. She visualized herself sinking into a warm darkness. Then she saw an image full of light, a little scene. She was in a kitchen somewhere, late in the afternoon with the sun angling in through the window. She was cooking something, and she sensed vaguely that children were moving about in the background. The phone was ringing. "Is Eldon Haller there?" someone was asking. "Well, Mrs. Haller, would you tell him for me—" And then Jenny was saying, very calmly, "I have a name."

"Excuse me," the other voice was saying, "is this the baseball player's wife?"

"No, I'm Jenny. Jenny Davis, the attorney."

But this was stupid. She had known all her life that she would get married someday and change her name. What did it matter? All the same, she felt almost angry. It all seemed so unfair.

She got up from the table, leaving half her milk sitting there, and went into the living room for her books. Then she walked to campus briskly, taking long strides. Once in the library, she settled down and studied.

In her literature class that morning she told her professor that she thought Milton was rather pompous and narrow-minded.

"My, my," the professor said, "we're feisty this morning, aren't we?"

Jenny shot him a little smile and said, "I don't know about you, but *I* am."

Chapter 8

Eldon's flight was scheduled for ten-forty the next morning, so he had little time to be with his family. One of his sisters had to hurry off to school early for drill-team practice, but he did have a few minutes to talk to his sister Barbara, a ninth-grader. He hardly knew what to say to her. She seemed to have grown up suddenly—was hardly the same girl he had known over the years—and he was such a little part of her life.

He was back on the plane before he even had a chance to enjoy the idea that he had been home. And now he kept remembering the little scene with his father at the breakfast table. He told his dad about the injury and what the doctor had said, actually just repeating what he had already said earlier over the telephone. His dad listened, hardly seeming to pay any attention, then said, "Eldon, I've been telling you all your life—you can do *anything* you want to do. *Anything*. You can come back from this shoulder thing."

Eldon nodded and glanced over at his mother. She looked a little concerned. "Yeah, I know, Dad. The only thing would be if it were torn worse than the doctor thinks. You know how hard Jeff Buttars tried to come back from his—"

"Now, come on," Dad said, pointing his fork at

Eldon, "let's not hear any of that kind of talk. You're not Jeff Buttars—you're Eldon Haller. You're the best there is, and before you're finished you'll be the best that ever was." It sounded more like a command than a compliment.

Eldon drank some milk and didn't say anything. His mother said, "Did you hear that Albert Noble died?"

"No, I didn't. That's too bad."

"Well, not really. He's suffered something terrible for the last six months or so. I think Mary was kind of relieved."

Eldon nodded. Then they all ate quietly for a time. "Looks like the alfalfa's ready to cut," Eldon finally said.

His father glanced up. "Yes, and that's just one more thing. Lately, it seems like I can hardly keep up with everything."

"Dad, why don't you sell the farm? With all the roofing you're doing all the time, couldn't you just—"

"No. I'm not going to sell it."

Eldon wasn't sure this was the right time, but he went ahead anyway. "Dad, I've been thinking. I'd like to have a new house built for you and Mom. Maybe it could be built right here on the farm. It wouldn't have to be anything fancy, but I'd really like you to have a nicer place. And then if you want to hire someone to come in and cut your hay, and—"

"No, Eldon. We're doing fine."

"But Dad, why not? All this money should be as much yours as it is mine. Why shouldn't you be able to take it a little easier now?"

"No, Eldon. I said we're doing fine."

"But you also just said you can hardly keep up with everything."

"Well, that's just how life is. But I don't plan to be a burden to any of my kids."

"Burden? Dad, I have more money than I'll ever

need. It's not right for you to be out on those roofs all day and farming till you can't see at night."

"Listen, son, you went ahead and set up those college funds for the girls and for your nephews. And I appreciate that. But I don't need no help for myself. I'm doing just fine."

He got up from the table and left a little too abruptly. Eldon glanced quickly at his mother, who was shaking her head. Now, on the airplane, Eldon was seeing it all again, wondering what it would take to change his dad's mind, and just how much of what he was had come from that little home in Hooper, Utah.

When Eldon got back to Kansas City, the team was gone, off on a road trip to Boston and New York. He called John Keanon in Boston, and John said that he should join the team there so Cy could help him with his rehabilitation program. And so the next morning Eldon flew to Boston.

What Eldon didn't do was call Jenny. He was going to let her think. He was not going to beg her to marry him. He spent his days reading or browsing in bookstores, and he did a lot of running and exercising when he went to the stadium each day. He wanted to fill his time, not think too much. He had the feeling that his life was on hold, as though he were just waiting to take his next breath.

The Royals always seemed to have troubles in Boston. This trip they lost the first two games, and in the second game Hal Connolly pulled a hamstring muscle and had to be taken out. He had been hitting well, so this was another blow to the team. However, it did mean that Les Huntley got a chance to play. It was what he had been waiting for.

Les struck out both times at bat, and in the eighth

inning he missed his cut-off man on a throw from right field, costing a run. The Royals lost five to one. After the game Les was really down. In the locker room, when Becker told him to try a new technique called "batting with your eyes open," he seemed to take it fairly well, but Eldon knew Les, and knew that he was hurting.

Eldon waited until the others left Les alone, then walked over to his dressing stall. "Should we go out to get something to eat?" he asked.

Les looked up and tried to smile. "I think I need something to *drink*." Les was from a strong Baptist family, and he didn't drink at all—which was one of the reasons he had been made Eldon's roommate.

Eldon laughed. "You might be right. Let's go get a root beer. Maybe two or three of 'em."

When they got back to the hotel, they went out to eat, and Eddie Hairton, another rookie who had just been called up to the majors, went with them. Eddie, a black from Los Angeles, was older than Eldon and Les, having played at USC and then a couple of years in the minors.

After the waiter took their order, Les slid his chair back, extending his legs. Barrel-chested and with a huge neck, he looked more like a linebacker than a baseball player. He might never win any Golden Glove awards for his defense, but a lot of people thought he was going to give Kansas City some of the power it had been lacking. He didn't look all that powerful right now, however, with dark hair drooping over his eyebrows and his eyes cast down.

"I really saw the ball well," he said. "I don't know what I'm doing wrong."

"You were trying too hard to pull the ball," Eldon said. "Everybody does that the first time they see that big green wall in Fenway Park. It's just sitting there so close that it looks like an easy shot."

"Listen, Les," Eddie said, "Valdez was striking out

guys when you were in grade school. You're not playing sandlot ball anymore; you're looking at the best."

"I know. That's just the problem. It makes me wonder if I can . . ." He didn't finish his sentence.

"If you can what?" Eldon asked.

"Well, I'm just not sure I can make it."

Eldon laughed. "Let's see. I think you're the first
rookie who ever asked himself that question."

Les continued looking at the table, or maybe just
below it. "Look, I know that," he said, "but it's easy for
you to say that now. You've made it. If I had your abil-
ity I could—"

"What are you talking about? I'm the guy without
an arm."

"It's going to get better, and then you'll—"

"Listen, you two," Eddie said, "I didn't come over
here to hear you guys cry all over each other. You both
have a better shot than I do. The way I look at it, at least
I got one good look around in the majors. If I make it,
great, and if I don't, I got a lot further than a lot of guys
I know."

"I wish I could look at it that way," Les said. "I
grew up in a little town, and everybody knows me.
This is the biggest thing that ever happened in my
town. There's an article in the paper about me almost
every night. If I don't make it now—well, I just *have* to
make it."

"You can't do that to yourself," Eldon said.

Just then a man walked up to their table, accom-
panied by a boy maybe thirteen or fourteen years old.

"Aren't you fellows with the Royals?" the man
asked. He was looking at Eldon.

"Yes, sir."

"You're Eldon Haller, aren't you?"

"Yes." It was the usual pattern. The man wanted
an autograph "for his son," but he seemed more interested than the boy. Eldon signed, and he asked the
young man whether he played ball, and wished him

success. "You better get these other guys to sign too," Eldon said. "These are the rookie *sensations*, Eddie Hairton and Les Huntley." The boy, with no apparent enthusiasm, nodded, and Eldon passed the slip of paper over to Les. "You probably heard about Les coming off the bench to inspire the Royals in their great play tonight."

Les glanced at Eldon, and then he grinned, showing his blunt teeth. "Yeah, I'm the one who kept the stadium cooled off by fanning with my bat."

"I'll tell you what, though," Eldon added, "Les is about to turn things around. And he's going to start tomorrow night. I'll tell you what he's going to do. Remember how Babe Ruth got up that time and pointed to center and then hit the home run out there? You know, for the sick kid. You've seen that old movie, haven't you?"

"Sure," the boy said.

"Okay. Tomorrow night Les Huntley, the famous rookie star, is going to step up to the plate and point to the big green wall out in left field, and he's—"

"Come on, Hooper," Les said, but he was still grinning.

"No, really. He's going to do it. He'll point to that left-field wall. And then—just for *you*—he's going to . . . punch a single into right."

The man laughed, and the boy looked sort of embarrassed. "Well, we'll be listening," the father said.

"No, you've got to be there. Tell me your name again. I'll have two box seats for you at the will-call window tomorrow night."

"Come on, Eldon," Les said, looking a little more sober.

"No, Les, you're going to do it." The man seemed not to be taking the offer seriously, but Eldon took his name and assured him the tickets would be there.

"Well, actually," the man said, "you don't have to—"

"No, listen. Les can do it. Just because he never touched the ball tonight, that doesn't mean a thing. In batting practice I've seen him hit balls clear out of the infield."

"That's right," Eddie said. "In his neighborhood the kids always chose him first."

"Well, all right. We'll be there," the man said.

"Great." Eldon looked at the boy. "And Jerry, you be ready for a big thrill."

"Hey, really," Les said, looking now at the boy, "come out to the game and everything, but, you know, they're just putting you on. I can't really do something like that."

"Of course you can, slugger. Don't be so modest," Eldon said, patting him on the back.

After the boy and his father left, Les told Eldon and Eddie they were a couple of jerks, but the two of them thought it was a wonderful idea.

"I can see him now," Eddie said, "gazing out to left field, then thrusting his finger out toward the wall. The crowd will rise to their feet and stare out to see what he's pointing at. And then—thunk—the ball will drop into right. It's going to be one of the great moments in sports. The thrill of victory, and all that sort of thing."

"Lay off, you guys," Les said. "I can't believe you'd tell that kid something like that. There's no way I'd pull such a dumb stunt."

"You can't let him down now, slugger. Didn't you tell me that the whole reason you had to do well in baseball was—" Eldon stopped, then said very slowly and distinctly, "to please everyone else?"

A long silence followed. Eventually Les nodded, looking at Eldon seriously. "Good point," he said. Eldon thought so too. But he couldn't help thinking about a certain man in Hooper, Utah—a man pointing a fork in Eldon's direction.

Chapter 9

The next night in Boston, when Les went to the plate, the whole team was waiting to see what would happen. Eddie and Eldon had told some of the team members about the incident in the restaurant, and somehow Becker had found out. Now everyone knew. And when Les did—sort of offhandedly—gesture toward left field, the players went nuts. Becker was yelling about the next Babe Ruth being at bat, and all the Royals were standing up, shouting and applauding. The Boston players must have wondered what in the world was happening.

When Les hit a weak grounder to the right side, he took a lot of heat from his teammates, but he handled it well. He seemed much more at ease than the night before. When he made a nice running catch in the second inning, he came back and told Becker, "Well, the Babe was a great hitter, but not as much of a glove man as some guys."

And the next time Les went to bat, he really did point. There was no mistaking it. He stood by home plate and then twisted and pointed directly at the big green wall. Becker and the other players went wild, falling all over each other, laughing and cheering. Becker stepped out of the dugout and yelled, "Get ready, Boston fans, the great Babe Huntley is about to launch one." John Keanon told him to get back in the dugout and shut his mouth, and he told the other players to lay off, but he didn't seem all that upset. He seemed to be enjoying what was happening himself.

Les took a pitch outside for a ball, then stepped out of the batter's box and pointed to left again. This time he gave it a real Babe Ruth flair, holding his position for three or four seconds. Eldon couldn't believe it. He was watching the crowd, and they seemed baffled. People were talking to each other, obviously wondering what was going on, and some were looking out to left, as though they thought Les wanted them to see something out there. When the umpire told Les to get back in the batter's box, the Royals all went nuts again.

The pitcher stayed outside with the next pitch, maybe thinking Les really did want to pull the ball. Les went with the pitch anyway, and hit it to right—really crunched it. It wasn't the single he had promised, but it cleared the right-field fence, so no one was complaining. It was Huntley's first major-league home run, and as he came trotting around the bases, he grinned from ear to ear and shook a clenched fist. The whole team was waiting for him at home plate. The Boston fans—and the players—were still wondering what was happening.

This was a turning point for Les. He seemed to relax after that, and he continued to hit well in the next series against the Yankees. In fact, he had plenty to do with the Royals' winning two of those three games.

Eldon was also doing better. He was working hard, and he could gradually feel some of the snap coming back into his arm. He practiced throwing the ball every day, and he was becoming confident that everything was going to be all right.

While he was in New York Eldon decided to call Jenny. He didn't push for any answers; he just wanted to talk. Jenny seemed happy to hear from him, and

Eldon liked that. She said that she could hardly wait to get home, which made him feel he had done the right thing by not sobbing over her or calling her every night to see whether she had made up her mind.

The next week, after the team returned to Kansas City, Jenny called Eldon. She told him she'd made a reservation to fly home and asked if he could come to the airport to get her. All week Eldon was building up a little fantasy that she had something to say to him. He could see her getting into his car, nestling close to him, and then saying, "Eldon, I've made up my mind. Let's get married—soon."

When Jenny's flight came in, Eldon was standing at the gate waiting for her. She was wearing jeans and a simple yellow blouse, and she looked very good. She had gotten some sun the last couple of weeks, and her coloring looked rich and healthy. Eldon also saw the softness in her eyes he had hoped for.

A couple of teenagers, a girl and a boy, had been standing with Eldon, talking about the Royals. They stepped back when Jenny approached, and now, as Eldon and Jenny walked away, they said good-bye. At the baggage pick-up, just as Jenny was telling Eldon about the flight, a man walked up and wanted to know about the progress of Eldon's shoulder. And again, as they were walking out of the terminal, another man stopped them and asked Eldon almost the same thing.

"Some things never change," Jenny said. "Missouri is still humid in the summer, and Eldon Haller can't walk five steps without one of his fans stopping him to check on his health."

"They mean well," Eldon said. "For a lot of people it's a big deal to talk to a professional athlete."

"I know how they feel, Hooper, my boy. I think it's a big deal too. Especially when the professional athlete hardly ever calls any more."

Eldon didn't say anything, but he was pleased. He

could hardly wait to get to the car. When they got there, however, and were finally sitting together in his little red Datsun, nothing was quite the way he pictured it. Jenny didn't snuggle up to him, but then, that would have been difficult with the bucket seats. And she was talking about her flight again, about the bumpy weather over the Rockies, and the gabby woman who had sat next to her.

Eldon drove to the exit and stopped to pay the parking fee. "Jenny," he said as they pulled on through the gate, "I'm sorry about not calling more. I told you when I was out there that I wanted you to think things over, and I just wanted to give you time—without pressure."

"I know. I appreciate that." She seemed to mean it, but then she became very quiet and subdued.

Eldon had been trying to give her a lead that might move the conversation in the right direction, but nothing happened. He didn't push the matter. "How were finals?"

"Not that hot. I did okay, I guess."

"Are you going back out for summer graduation?"

"We might. My parents said they'd like to go."

Eldon felt a little awkward, and Jenny seemed to feel the same way. They were on the freeway now, passing through rolling hills. "It's nice to be home," Jenny said.

"Does it seem like home to you, Jenny?"

"Sure it does. I like Utah, but this is still my home."

"When I was in Hooper that last time, it really hit me that I don't have a home anymore."

"Well, with all your traveling it's been hard for you to get to know all that many people around here. Do you ever hear from Mac?"

"Once in a while. He looks me up when he's in town sometimes. He's still going to college over in Warrensburg, and this summer he's down at the Lake of the Ozarks."

"You ought to talk your dad into moving out here, Eldon. You're a home boy. You need your family."

Eldon couldn't believe she would say something like that. It was like admitting that she didn't see herself as the one to give him a family. "He would never do that," he said, struggling not to show how stung he was by her remark.

Jenny seemed to know she'd said the wrong thing. She put her hand on his shoulder. "How's the arm feeling?"

"Okay."

"Is it really?"

"Yes. I'm going to pitch a few innings next week. I'm almost back to normal." But his voice wasn't quite normal, as much as he was trying to make it sound that way.

He turned on the radio, then glanced over at Jenny. She was looking straight ahead, sitting a little too erect.

"Listen, Jenny, I have the feeling we're both a little uptight. Until I know what you've decided, it's hard to relax."

"I know," she said. "Until *I* know what I've decided it's hard for me too."

"So you haven't made up your mind yet?"

"No."

"Don't you have to let the law school know?"

"Well, yes. I accepted, just in case. But if I'm going to change my mind, I really should let them know right away."

The anger in Eldon was rising now, but he didn't want her to know that. "Jenny," he said, "I want you to make up your mind. This is getting to be . . . difficult."

"I know, Eldon. It isn't easy for me either. I've made up my mind twenty times in the past couple of weeks, but every time I decide one way, I immediately start to feel a terrible loss of the other."

"That doesn't say much for how you feel about me."

"But Eldon, it does. If I didn't feel so much for you, the whole thing would be easy."

"Oh, come on, Jenny." He could feel himself slipping toward words he might regret, but he was starting not to care. "You've had four years of college. Is going back for more really *that* important right now?"

"Eldon, don't. Okay?" He looked over at her, wondering what that was supposed to mean. She hurried on. "We need to talk. I need to explain to you how I feel about all this. I just think we—"

"What about how *I* feel, Jenny? I thought we had an understanding. We've been talking about getting married this summer for at least two years."

"I know, but I just didn't realize that—"

"Look, Jenny, I just want you to decide." He had let his voice get too loud, and now he tried to bring it back into control. "I think it's time for us to get married if we're going to. I've already told you that you can go to law school here, and I'll support you in that."

Jenny sat silent for a time. "Eldon," she finally said, "I told you before that I don't think it would work out very well for us to get married while I'm still trying to go to school. But I think we need to talk this all out. That's why I came home before I made a decision."

"Jenny, I'm sorry, but I have a hard time believing that. I think you're just stalling again. When it comes right down to it, you'll make up your own mind." He almost missed his exit and had to hurry to change lanes. He came into the exit a little too fast, the tires squealing as he looped around the long turn. "I have some pride, Jenny. I don't think I should have to beg you to marry me."

"What are you talking about?"

As they came out of the cloverleaf and onto a city street, Eldon pulled the car over to the side. He wanted to look at her. "Jenny, how do you think it makes me feel to have you playing these games: 'Do I want him, or don't I? Oh, gee, this is so tough. Maybe I'd rather stay in school—maybe not.'" His tone was a mocking one. Then he stopped, took a breath, and said more quietly, "Believe it or not, there are some women around who wouldn't have to think quite so long if I asked them to marry me. I don't have to play this game forever. I want a commitment from you, Jenny. I want it now."

"Well, Eldon, I came home trying to find my answer." She had still been looking out the front window, but now she turned and looked at him. "You're making it very easy for me. Maybe you'd better go propose to one of those women who's just *waiting* to marry Mr. Superstar." There was acid in her voice.

Suddenly Eldon lost control. "Thanks," he said. "You finally gave me a straight answer. And now you won't have to suffer any longer." He snapped the clutch out and the car shot forward. He drove too fast for several blocks and made a hard right turn into Jenny's street. In front of Jenny's house he stopped the car abruptly, then hopped out. She slowly opened the door on the other side and got out as he lifted the hatchback and pulled out her suitcases. Then he set them on the grass next to the curb, got back in the car, and blasted out again. He didn't want to say another word.

In the rearview mirror he could see Jenny's mother standing on the front steps, looking confused, as Jenny picked up her bags, not even watching him drive away. It was a little scene he would see in his mind many times in the next few weeks. But right now he was just getting out of there, driving faster than he should, trying hard to hate her, hating himself much more. What he didn't want to do, however, was feel regret. Anger was much more comforting for the moment.

Chapter 10

Jenny trudged up the front lawn toward the house. "What in the world?" her mother was saying.

"That's what's known as an exit scene, Mom."

"What happened?"

"He drove away—fast."

"Jenny, I'm serious. What happened?"

"I'm not sure I even know."

"Well, did you get in a fight?"

Jenny looked at her mother. She always looked surprisingly older these days—not older than the time before, but older than some time in the past, some time that remained in Jenny's mind. "Yes, I guess that's what you'd call it."

"But why?"

Jenny set the suitcase down. "Let's start over, okay? Hi, Mom, it's sure nice to be home. Glad to see you."

"Jenny, don't."

"I just don't feel like talking about it right now, Mom. Okay?" She turned and walked back to get her two smaller bags.

Her mother stayed where she was, on the steps. "Jenny," she said, "I don't know what's happened, but I hope you'll—"

"Mom, the whole thing is over with. I've finally made up my mind. I'm going to law school this fall."

She tried to walk past, but her mother reached out and took her by the shoulders and turned her so they faced each other. "Jenny, don't do this. I think you're making a big mistake."

"I know. I suspect I am. And I'm sure everyone in the world would agree with you."

"Then why do it?"

Jenny didn't answer. She wanted to. She wanted to explain how she felt, but she really didn't think her mother would understand. Wasn't it obvious: how could any girl in her right mind pass up a guy like Eldon? He wasn't just the all-American boy—he was a millionaire.

Jenny took the two little bags upstairs to the room that had once been her own and left the big suitcase out on the lawn. She didn't want to go back down and face her mother right now, or any of the family who might be around.

She stood at the window and looked out on the city skyline, and then she started to get angry with herself for being so depressed. She wasn't going to let this happen. She had made her decision. Now that it was made, she was going to stand by it, and she wasn't going to second-guess herself.

She flipped open one of her bags and found Eldon's picture on top. The cover was closed, but she could see the picture clearly in her mind. Then she sat down on the bed and started to cry—just this once. She was going to allow herself to cry once, and that would be it.

Chapter 11

For the next few days, Eldon poured himself into his training, trying to concentrate on his upcoming pitching assignment. He promised himself he was not going to sit around and mope about Jenny Davis. He had let himself worry about her far too long. What he wanted now was to pitch well. He needed that part of his life to straighten out; then everything else would follow.

He also wanted to get a date with someone else. He had only occasionally dated others besides Jenny, and that, he now felt, had been a mistake. Now he was going to meet some other women, and actually the prospect was rather exciting. In a way it felt good to know that the whole experience with Jenny was finally over; now he could have the fun of starting something new, and maybe this time he would find a woman who was really more suited to him.

Eldon had noticed a young woman at church the past few weeks. He remembered her from the summer before, and he knew she had been at BYU all winter, but he didn't know her name. What he did know was that she was a real knockout. She had beautiful long hair, the color of varnished oak, and a ravishing smile. Someone said she'd been runner-up to the homecoming queen at BYU; Eldon could only wonder what the winner had looked like.

Added to the rest, she had been giving Eldon a good deal of attention. One Sunday she'd come over to talk to him before he left for the stadium. She'd told him how much she loved sports, especially baseball, and that it was really a thrill to meet him. Eldon had heard that sort of thing from plenty of other people, but, unlike many, she didn't seem star-struck. She was very much in control, very smooth and confident. She really did seem happy to meet him, and Eldon had thought even then that he wouldn't mind asking her out some time.

On the Sunday after his break-up with Jenny, he did a little more investigating. He found out she had just finished her junior year at BYU. Her father, who was on the stake high council, was apparently very well-to-do. Eldon had asked a newly returned missionary about her and found out her name was Debbie Larsen. "Man, she's out of my class," the other man had said, "but Eldon, you'd have it made. Every girl I've met here wants to know how she can get a chance to meet you. They're so jealous of the bishop's daughter they can hardly stand it."

Eldon saw the "bishop's daughter" only from a distance, and he avoided her parents. Gary, Jenny's younger brother, did come over and ask him whether he felt ready to pitch. "Well, yeah," Eldon said. "I feel pretty much back to full strength." But he was self-conscious.

"Well, good luck," Gary said. "I hope everything goes all right for you."

It sounded terribly final, as though Gary were saying, "Since I won't be seeing you again . . ."

Eldon tried to hurry away right after priesthood meeting, but Debbie was standing by the door again. She flashed that smile at him and said, "Hi, Eldon." He slowed down, tried to say something but couldn't think of anything, and then just said hello and walked on. But that evening he looked up her number in the stake directory and called her.

A woman who was obviously older answered. "Sister Larsen," Eldon said, "is Debbie home?"

"Yes, she is. May I say who's calling?"

"This is Eldon Haller."

"Oh—the baseball player?"

"Yes, ma'am."

"Well, well. Just a moment. I'll call Debbie."

What was "well, well" supposed to mean? Eldon wondered.

"Hello, Eldon?"

"Debbie, this is . . . or, I mean, yes. Say, I was wondering . . . you mentioned that you liked baseball."

"Yes, I surely do."

What a voice! Eldon wasn't sure he was ready for this. "Well, I'm pitching again for the first time in quite a while, and I—"

"Yes. On Tuesday. I read that in the paper this morning."

"I just thought you might like to go to the game. I can get you a box seat. Then afterwards, if you wanted to, maybe we could get something to eat—if you don't mind eating that late."

"Eldon, that sounds marvelous. You must have seen how lonely I looked and decided to take pity on me."

"Well, no. I—"

"What time should I be ready?"

"You could go over with me—early—and watch the teams take batting practice, or—"

"That sounds great."

"Well, good. That means I'll have to pick you up about four-thirty, though. Are you working this summer?"

"No, no. I'm free as a bird. Four-thirty is fine."

"Okay, then. I have your address. I guess it hasn't changed, has it?"

"Oh, no. We've lived in the same old place for years."

"Good. I'll find it."

"I'll see you on Tuesday, then. And Eldon, thank you so much for asking me. I'm really excited."

"Oh, sure. Well, good-bye then."

"Bye-bye."

As Eldon put down the phone, he caught his breath. He hoped he would learn to relax around Debbie. But right now he felt as though he needed to send out his tongue and have it pressed.

On Tuesday Eldon picked up Debbie at her house, which turned out to be something of a palace. Brother Larsen showed up in a three-piece suit, saying he had come home early for once. It was never exactly clear whether he had done that so he could meet Eldon or whether it was just a coincidence. But he welcomed Eldon into the house and trotted out a nice little herd of well-dressed kids of varying ages. They were all very polite as they shook hands with Eldon. As it turned out, they were all going to the game that night, and Eldon apologized several times for not getting tickets for everyone.

"Oh, not at all," Brother Larsen kept saying, "we try to go a few times each summer, and we're overdue this year."

"We'll be cheering for you, Eldon," Sister Larsen said, flashing remarkably straight teeth—virtually the same set that her daughter had.

Eldon was relieved when he got out of there, but he was almost speechless. Debbie had suddenly appeared before him in orange pants and an orange and white striped top. Her hair, streaming down her back, was full of golden highlight tones. He felt his face getting hot and knew he was blushing, but she took hold of his arm as though she had known him for years. She seemed completely relaxed.

In the car on the way to the stadium, he found that she knew how to make things easy. She thought of things to say and asked questions, trying to put Eldon at ease. The conversation seemed a little calculated, but it showed some grace. Once they got past this initial unfamiliarity, Eldon thought she would be nice to be around. He glanced over at her, sneaking a look. Oh, man, if the other players saw her, they would never let him live it down. But what did he care? If she had a spirit that was even half as nice . . .

As Eldon took Debbie to her box seat, he noticed the ushers taking second and third looks. By the time he got to the dressing room he was so preoccupied with thoughts of Debbie that he realized he had hardly thought about the game. And that was very strange for Eldon. Maybe it was a good sign. Maybe his confidence had returned and he would be able to relax and get back to his old form.

All through warm-ups Eldon continued to feel good. His arm was loosening nicely. Jimmy Kirk, the catcher who warmed him up, said that he had good stuff, almost as good as the year before when he had been at his best.

By the time he stepped to the mound to face the first batter, the park was almost full, unusual for a Tuesday night. They were there to see whether their young star was ready to go now. Eldon felt that he was. And the Cleveland Indians were believing it too before a couple of innings had gone by.

Eldon moved the ball around, constantly picking up the edges of the plate, never giving the batter anything down the middle. He changed speeds enough that his fast ball, when he put something on it, seemed faster than it really was. He still didn't feel powerful, but he felt in control.

He gave up his first hit in the fourth inning, a single, and then he faced the number-three batter, who had been swinging a hot bat of late. He made a good pitch, a slider down and away. The batter hit a weak grounder right back to Eldon, and he spun and threw to second base. Lincoln turned it into an easy double play. A roar rolled down out of the stands, and Eldon walked off the mound feeling he had returned home. He had missed this sense of mastery the past few weeks. Making a baseball do what he wanted it to do was the one thing he had always been sure of. He loved the quiet that came over the stadium before an important pitch, and the explosion of joy when he struck someone out. It was like being the conductor of an orchestra, his arm directing the response. No wonder he'd felt so empty lately.

From the bench he watched Debbie, who was sitting near the third-base line. She seemed very involved. Some of the players had seen Eldon talking to her before the game. Becker had some less-than-dainty things to say, and so did some of the other guys, but Les came over now and said, "Did you really bring that chick over there to the game?" Eldon nodded, trying not to smile. "Wow, Hooper, I didn't think you had it in you. Are you sure you're safe with her? Maybe you'd better take me along just to—"

"Listen, Les, she's a nice Mormon girl. She goes to BYU. She just looks—well, you know—she's just pretty."

"Pretty? Hooper, that girl is in some other league from 'pretty.'"

When Eldon walked back to the mound, he felt very good. He still wasn't pitching his best, but he was doing the right things, getting people out. In the fifth inning he let a couple of pitches get out over the plate and he gave up two hits, but considering how long he'd been out of the rotation, that didn't worry him. He got out of the inning with no damage done, and the Royals scored three runs right after that, giving him a four-to-nothing lead.

In the sixth, however, Eldon got a pitch up and Paul Waite slammed it into the left-field corner for a double. After that, big Steve Adams came up and muscled a fast ball clear to the wall in center. The run scored and Adams went all the way around to third.

Keanon came out of the dugout immediately. On the way out he motioned for a left-hander, and Eldon wasn't surprised. Before the game they'd agreed that he probably wouldn't pitch more than five or six innings. "You're looking good—not bad at all, Hooper," Keanon said. "I couldn't have hoped for anything better than this. Is the shoulder starting to bother you?"

"No, not at all. I still can't seem to get quite as much on my fast ball as I want to—but I'm not too far away."

"That's good, Hooper. If we can hang onto this lead tonight, we might look back to this game later on and see it as a turning point in our whole season. It means an awful lot to the guys to know you're back."

Eldon nodded. He glanced over toward the box seats. He had told Debbie he probably wouldn't pitch too long tonight. He hoped she understood why he was coming out of the game.

Eldon walked off the mound and the crowd gave him a huge ovation. Eldon liked it. He felt very happy. A burden was lifting—maybe a couple of them.

As he walked into the dugout, Becker said, "Hey, Hooper, you look tired. You'd better let me give that little honey of yours a ride home. I'm not sure you can drive safely."

"I *know* she's safer with me than with you," Eldon said, and he continued on by. "You guys keep that lead," he added as he entered the tunnel that led to the clubhouse.

And they did. They even enlarged it, winning

seven to two. By the time the other players came tromping into the team room, Eldon was dressed. He wanted to get away as quickly as he could and not leave Debbie waiting too long. But he was soon surrounded by reporters, and he knew better than to try to push them aside. He answered questions for twenty minutes or so before he said, "I really have to go tonight, you guys."

Becker, of course, had some comments to make about that, but Eldon managed to get out. He found Debbie waiting at the elevator doors upstairs, where he had asked her to meet him.

She grabbed his arm immediately. "Oh, Eldon," she said, "aren't you excited? You were *so* great."

"Well, I was satisfied. I couldn't quite—"

"Oh, am I hurting your arm? I shouldn't—"

"I pitch with the other one," he said, and for some reason he could feel himself blushing.

"Oh, that's right—stupid me. Well, I'll take whichever one you can spare. Okay?"

"You can have them both if you want," Eldon said, trying to sound relaxed. She smiled, and then she nestled close to him, squeezing his arm against her side. Eldon took a deep breath.

They were about to walk away when the elevator doors opened and some of the players got off, Les leading the way. "Oh, hi, Hooper. Is this the date you told us about?" He looked her over carefully. "Gee, I don't know. She doesn't look to me like someone you took out as a favor to her mother. Why did you tell us that?"

Debbie took this right in stride. "Well, someone had to take pity on me," she said, and then she let loose her dazzling smile.

Eldon introduced her then, rather awkwardly.

"You'd better hang on to old Hooper," Les said. "He's quite the ladies' man. He's got a different chick out here every night."

"Is that so?" Debbie said. "Well, maybe I'll just hold on and fight the others off." She pulled his arm closer against her. It was a squeeze to remember, and Eldon felt his face getting hot again.

"Hey, look," Les said, "why don't we double sometime—and I'll get someone for Eldon to go out with."

Debbie laughed. "Now, why would I want to do that?"

Les was starting to seem a little nervous, or maybe he was just struggling to think of something else to say. "Has Hooper ever hit a home run for you?"

"Well, no. He hasn't done that."

"I'll tell you what. Next time I get in the game, I'll point to left and hit a home run to right. It's something I do for certain very good friends."

"That sounds really great," Debbie said. "I'll tell you what. If you can do that, I'll line you up with a girl I know. I owe her mother a favor."

The other players had been standing back, letting Les play his games, but they cracked up at this. Les had certainly met his match—and then some.

A big crowd, mostly kids, was waiting when they came out of the stadium. They were getting signatures from other players, but when Eldon came out, most of them rushed toward him. Debbie stepped back a little and let them have him for the moment. It took at least ten minutes to get away, but every time Eldon looked her way, she was beaming with pleasure.

When they finally managed to escape to the car, she seemed excited. "I can't believe what that must be like, Eldon. Those kids worship you. Isn't it thrilling?"

"In a way, I guess. But I get tired of it. It would be nice if people didn't notice me quite so much."

He looked at her. She was sitting back against the door, turned toward him. Though there wasn't much light in the parking lot, he could see that she really was beautiful, with perfect features and such pretty hair.

And she seemed nice, too. Her looks gave people the wrong impression. Maybe she was the kind of person he had been needing all along. For one thing, she really seemed to believe in him.

"Thanks, Hooper," she said softly, and his nickname sounded nice on her lips.

"For what?"

"For asking me out. For bringing me with you on such a special night." She reached over and took hold of his hand, and then she brushed a little kiss along the back of it. Chills ran all the way up his back. It took him several seconds to remember how to start the car.

Chapter 12

"Dad, I don't see what point there is in talking again. We'll just say the same things we said last week—and the week before that."

"I'm the bishop. I'm used to saying the same things over and over." He was smiling, but Jenny wasn't. She really didn't want this. The only good thing about her life right now was that her mind was made up.

Bishop Davis came in and sat down on the chair by the door, and he swung the door shut. Jenny was sitting on the bed, her back against the headboard. She had been reading, but she put the book down. "What're you reading?" her father asked.

"*Light in August.*"

"What?"

"It's a Faulkner novel."

"Is it good?"

"I guess so. I just started it."

"Are you okay?"

"Yes, Dad. I'm fine. Really."

He stood up and undid his tie, then pulled his suit coat off and threw it on the bed. When he sat down again, he turned the little chair around backwards and sat with his legs spraddled and his arms resting on the chair back. "Then how come you sit up here and read all the time? Every summer you've been home before, you've been out playing tennis most of the time, or working—or something. You hardly even come down in the evenings to talk to anyone."

It was evening, and the bishop had just come home from a Church meeting. The room was sinking into soft shadows. Jenny had needed more light for the past several minutes, but she wasn't really reading anyway—she was staring at the page. "Well, obviously, I'm not in any singing and dancing mood, Dad. But that's partly because of the way you and Mom have reacted. If I had my way, I'd be back in Provo right now looking for work. You're the one who said I should stay here for a while."

"That's because I wanted to repeat the same conversation a few more times before you leave me forever. It's better than nothing."

"Is that what you're afraid of, Dad? That I'm getting to be too independent?"

He laughed and then put his forehead on his arms. "Oh, Jenny," he said, still looking down, "you were independent the day we brought you home from the hospital." He looked up again. "But that still doesn't make it easy to see you leave this way."

"I don't get it, Dad. I've been going off to BYU every fall for four years. What's so different all of a sudden?"

"You know that as well as I do, sis."

"No, I don't. I really don't. I'll probably come home next summer. I just want to go to school three more years. I don't see that it's so different from going for the first four."

"You always accepted my money before," he said, smiling. There was a good-natured quality about Dad that Jenny always found disarming. He'd never been the disciplinarian in the family—that had been left to Mom. He had a subtle, almost shy way of smiling that had always elicited smiles from Jenny.

But Jenny didn't smile now. "Dad, I can't do that anymore. You have Rosemary in college now, and everyone else coming up. It's not fair to accept your help for more than four years."

"Well, actually, I guess I agree with you. But it's one thing to turn *you* down, and it's another to have you turn *me* down. It has separated us. I'm not having a very easy time dealing with that, Jenny. And the truth is, I don't see how you're going to manage."

"I've thought about that, Dad. I know I won't be able to work all that much, but I can borrow. You've always said that education was one thing worth investing in, even if it hurts at times. Once I get out and in a practice, I can—"

"That's the other thing."

"What?"

"Jenny, do you really want to be a lawyer?"

"Yes, Dad, I do."

"Why?"

"Why shouldn't I? I don't see that being a woman should have anything to do with it."

"Jenny, I didn't say that it did. I want to know why *you* want to be a lawyer."

"Dad, if Gary wanted to go into law, you'd shout for joy. You wouldn't stop for a moment to ask him why. It's because you think of me as your little girl that you start asking all the questions."

Bishop Davis didn't say anything for a time. He took off his glasses and rubbed the side of his nose. "Well, I'll admit, you have a point. I think that's probably true. Nonetheless, I probably should ask Gary just as much as I am asking you. So I'm still asking. Why do you want to be a lawyer?"

"Well—in the first place, I think I have a good mind. I want to do something with it. I want to train it, sharpen it. I want to *use* it."

"Why in law?"

"I just think law is a good field to train me in analysis and careful thinking. It's a good, basic degree that leaves a lot of different directions open."

"So it's law school more than *being* a lawyer that attracts you?"

Jenny sat thinking. She was almost veiled in darkness now. "I guess that's right," she finally said. "I don't know that I have any great cause to fight for, or that I feel excited about any particular branch of the law. It's the training itself that I want more than anything."

"Could that possibly mean that what you want is extended schooling more than a career?"

Jenny was interested in this question. Her father was getting at something. "I really don't know, Dad. I just can't see that far ahead right now."

"Do you want to get married—sooner or later?"

"Of course I do."

"And do you want to have kids?"

"Yes."

"How are you going to make it all work, Jenny?"

"Dad, now we're getting right back to the circle we've been going around ever since I got home. I don't know the answer to that."

"But that's just it, Jenny. You can't live out the next three years without facing the implications of your choice."

"But Dad, I'll only be twenty-five. Maybe a lot of women worry about getting that old before they get married—but I don't. I started college with your firm advice not to get married until I finished; now all of a sudden you make it sound like life or death if I don't get married right now."

"Nicely put," he said. Jenny could see him nod. "I guess, in some ways, I have made an awful lot out of your education, and now I'm sort of . . . well . . ."

"You're saying, 'That's all very well, little girl, but enough's enough.'"

"Let's leave out the 'little girl' part."

"Okay—but Dad, you don't understand what

you've done to me. All my life you've been telling me how important it is to get an education, and then all of a sudden, you say, 'Now don't get carried away. Just because you're educated doesn't mean you ought to *do* something with it. Now settle down and get married, and just hang your diploma on the wall so everyone will know you're not stupid.'"

"That's not quite fair, Jenny. I want you to have a trained mind, and I do want you to *use* it. But that doesn't change the fact that your role should be to marry and raise a family. I've been teaching you that forever too, Jenny."

"I know, Dad. But you forgot to tell me how to do both at the same time." They sat silent for some time after that. Jenny was feeling worse. The dilemma was all too real without her father clarifying it for her one more time. "Dad," she eventually said, "I still don't see the difference in waiting for three more years. Twenty-five isn't too old to get married. Maybe I'll meet someone in law school."

"Things pass by, Jenny. If it weren't for Eldon, I'd say fine. But I don't see how you can just throw away—"

Suddenly Jenny was angry. She slid off her bed and walked to the window, turning her back. "Dad, this is the part we've been over and over. I don't want to talk about it anymore."

"All right, Jenny. But you can't blame parents for trying when they think one of their children is making a big mistake."

"I understand that. Oh, do I understand! I've heard it from everyone: poor, stupid Jenny is missing her chance to marry a millionaire. What a loss."

"Jenny, don't give me that. This family loves Eldon, and we have for a long time. His money has nothing to do with it. Do you think I'd want you to marry someone I didn't consider worthy of you, just because he had money?"

Jenny was calming down a little. Her family did

genuinely like Eldon; she knew that was true. And she didn't blame them. "Okay, Dad, I admit that." She took a long breath. "I'm going to try to tell you why I don't want to marry him. You may not like my reasons, but at least you'll know what they are. And the truth is, I know they wouldn't make sense to many people, and probably not to you."

"Try me."

"Dad, Eldon is Mr. Everything—superstar, rich, handsome—"

"And a fine young man."

"Okay, that's true. And he's not impressed with himself, and he's understanding and loving, and he would make a wonderful husband and father."

"It's going to take some kind of flaw to cancel all that out, Jenny."

"There is no such flaw. I mean, he has his problems, and he can be very irritating—but basically you're right. There's no flaw to cancel out all that's good about him."

"And so?"

"Dad, if I marry him—now—I will become *Mrs. Superstar*. Reporters will ask me what he eats for breakfast and whether he's pleasant around the house. Someone will ask me to do a commercial with him on television, and I'll get to say something wonderful like, 'Hooper and I use them all the time.' Do you see what I mean, Dad? I look at my alternatives. One is to go on to school and to challenge my mind, to grow some more and find out what I'm really capable of doing. The other is to disappear, to get swallowed up. I want to have a husband and a family, but I don't want to lose every shred of *self* in the process. It's not fair."

"But, Jenny, I think you have the wrong view of it. You know, you really sound quite selfish. When you become a mother, you give up plenty—there's no doubt about that. But that's God's plan to teach us not to always put ourselves first."

"Then why don't men have to give up anything?"

"Oh, Jenny, come on. If you think working every day is so great, then—"

"No, Dad. I'm not talking about working. I'm talking about *being*. Eldon doesn't have to give up baseball; why should I have to give up everything I would like to do? If I marry him, I'll have *his* money to spend, *his* reputation to share, *his* heroics to glory in— *his* life. But who will I be?"

Jenny stared out the window. The lights were coming on in the tall buildings downtown, but the city looked murky and gray.

"Look, Jenny, I think I do understand how you feel. But I don't think it has to be that way. You are who you are, and Eldon's not one to take that from you. You're strong, Jenny. You're going to do some things with your life; you'll be known for your own abilities."

"I don't have any yet, Dad. That's just the point. I won't marry Eldon till I have my own separate sense of who I am."

"But Jenny, that doesn't come from school. That comes from a lifetime of growth. You find yourself when you forget yourself."

Jenny heard his words, and they touched her. She thought about them for some time. Finally she said, "That's right, Dad. And I think that's really the point. I'm not ready to be married. I'm still too selfish. I need to get a few things out of my system first."

"But Eldon's not going to wait forever."

"I know. That's exactly what he said. Now you have the whole picture."

Bishop Davis stood up and took a step toward Jenny, then stopped. "Would you like to work in a law office the rest of the summer?" he said.

"What?"

"I talked to Brother Garnett tonight and told him you were planning to go to law school. He wondered if you would want to work for him, in his office, and get a feel for what the career is like."

"Is this some conspiracy to discourage me from going to law school?"

He smiled. "No, Jenny. It's putting you out to work so you won't be a burden to me in my old age."

He put his arms out, and Jenny came to him and hugged him. "Thanks, Dad."

He stepped back a little and looked at Jenny through the darkness: "Well, I'll tell you something. I was sort of proud to tell him you had been accepted. I even told him your exam scores, and he was very impressed."

Jenny merely nodded, but she was pleased. It was as though she had finally come home for the summer.

Chapter 13

Eldon saw Debbie several times during the week after their first date. A couple of times he picked her up late, after games, and they went out for something to eat, and one day he took her to lunch. She looked perfect every time. In fact, he decided he had better do something to keep pace. He needed some more clothes himself, and he had been driving the same little Datsun since he first came to Kansas City.

On the following Monday the Royals had a night off, and Eldon had a date scheduled with Debbie. That morning he drove out to the Independence Mall and bought himself a sport coat and a pair of slacks, some shirts and ties, and a pair of shoes. He had never bought such expensive clothes before, but he couldn't see any reason why he shouldn't.

Not long after he got back to his condo, early in the afternoon, the phone rang. It was his old friend Mac, who had been batboy with the team when Eldon first came up to the Royals. He wanted to know how Eldon's shoulder was doing.

"It's going to be all right, Mac. I'm pitching again Wednesday. John gave me a long rest again, and I feel as strong as ever."

"That's really great, Eldon. Hey, listen, when can

we get together? Do you have anything going tonight?"

"Well, yes, I do, Mac. I have a date." He thought
about asking Mac to get a date and join them, but he
felt a little uneasy about that. Debbie and Mac were
very different sorts.

"So Jenny must be in town, huh?"

Eldon sat down on the couch. "Well, yes, she is.
But I'm not going out with her anymore, Mac. I'm dating someone else."

"You've got to be kidding. Really?"

"Yeah. Really."

"What happened?"

Eldon didn't want to get into the whole thing.
"Well, I guess we broke up."

"What do you mean?"

"I don't know exactly. All of a sudden she decided
she wanted to go to law school. I'm just tired of the
whole situation. I think the woman I'm taking out now
is better for me."

"Better for you? She sounds like medicine."

"No, not at all. She's really beautiful, Mac."

"Well, to each his own, Hooper, but I don't know. I
think I'd trade all the women I know for one Jenny
Davis. Maybe you ought to give me her phone
number."

But Eldon didn't laugh. "Well, I don't know, Mac.
Sometimes things just don't work out."

"I guess," Mac said, and there was an awkward
pause. "But I have a hard time buying that. What's so
bad about her going to law school? You're only
twenty-one. What's the rush?"

This remark especially irritated Eldon, partly because it was embarrassing. "I know, Mac. But I've
been out here alone most of the time since I got out of
high school. It might be different if I were going to college full time."

"Well, Eldon, you have to play your own games, I

guess. But it sounds to me like your ego is hurt. You know how Jenny is—she never will be one to curl up at your feet at the end of a long day."

"I know, Mac. But maybe that's what I need."

"Oh, man, Eldon. If that's what you want, you deserve it. I'd take Jenny any day. I like to talk to a person who has something to say."

Eldon didn't want to go on with this. He wished he could just *show* Mac—just trot Debbie out and say, "Okay, take a look. Tell me you wouldn't want *that* curled up at your feet."

"Actually, Eldon, there was another reason I called. Do you still have that journal your great-grandfather wrote—the one who lived here in Jackson County?"

"Sure."

"Could I read it sometime?"

"Yeah. I'll have to dig it up. But sure, you can read it. Why?"

"Well, I just remember what an effect it had on you, and I thought I'd like to see what the man thought about. I've been on this kick lately, reading biographies and diaries—mostly by religious people."

"Mac, I swear, I don't know how you find the time."

"Well, I still get Cs in my classes and read everything but what I'm assigned. I don't have any idea what I'm majoring in. How's *your* reading going, Eldon? The last time I saw you, I gave you that big list of books."

"Yeah, well, I found most of them. I've read quite a few. But I don't go at it quite the way you do."

Eldon and Mac continued chatting for a while, and Mac said he would stop by the next day to pick up the journal. When Eldon got off the phone he decided he'd better see if he could find it. As it turned out, finding it was not a problem. His mistake was in sitting down and starting to read it. He got very involved, remembering some of the feelings and thoughts that had been lying dormant in him since the first time he'd read it. He read all afternoon, sometimes pausing for long stretches to think.

After one such long pause, he suddenly looked down at his watch and realized he was supposed to pick up Debbie in ten minutes. He took a quick shower and changed, then called to let Debbie know he was running late; but he was still half an hour late in getting to her house.

Debbie was ready when he arrived, wearing a beautiful turquoise dress, with matching shoes and eye shadow. Eldon could see that she had put on her makeup painstakingly; he was embarrassed to think how quickly he had dressed, and he found himself wondering if his tie was knotted correctly. As they walked to the car he apologized once again for being late. "Well, it doesn't matter to me that much," Debbie said. "I just hope we don't lose our reservations."

"Oh—I didn't make reservations. Don't you think on a Monday night we could get in without—"

"I doubt it, Eldon. Didn't you say you wanted to go to Carlton's?"

"Well, that's what I thought."

By now she was getting in the car. Eldon shut the door and walked around to the other side. As he got in, Debbie said, "Eldon, I really don't think we should try to show up at Carlton's without reservations. I doubt that anyone does that."

"Oh." The tension in her voice made Eldon nervous. "I've never been there. I guess I didn't realize it was quite so . . . you know . . ."

"Well, it's a *very* nice place, Eldon."

Eldon was waiting for the ease he had come to expect from her. "Look, Debbie, I'm really sorry. Maybe I could call down there right now. We could—"

"Let me," she said, and she got out of the car. Eldon sat where he was, feeling like some clod who had just wandered into town for the first time. But when she returned, she seemed more relaxed. "I had Daddy call. He knows the people there. He got you in, but he said you'd better give the captain an extra ten dollars, since he only made room for us as a special favor."

An *extra* ten? Eldon was beginning to wonder what he had gotten himself into. He wasn't worried about not having enough money; he just felt out of place. "Debbie, I feel really stupid. I didn't realize—"

"Oh, Eldon, don't be silly." He was pulling out of the long driveway. "Stop for just a second." He stopped the car, and she reached over and patted his cheek, then slid her hand around his neck, brushing his ear. She pulled his face toward her and gave him a quick kiss on the cheek. "Hooper," she whispered, "I'm the one who should be sorry. I had no reason to get upset. You couldn't help it, since you've never been there. Next time you'll know." She kissed him again, this time on the ear, breathing just enough to send chilling waves down his neck.

As it turned out, Eldon got by all right at Carlton's. In the first place, he went ahead and dished out plenty of money. He didn't know how much was appropriate, so he just gave a lot more than seemed necessary to the captain and the waiter, and they seemed satisfied, calling him Mr. Haller and bowing graciously.

It also turned out that the customers in Carlton's were just as likely to come to his table to meet him as were people in any restaurant in town. They were very classy about it, however, introducing themselves, wishing him well, and only as a sort of afterthought requesting autographs for their sons—all of whom seemed to be great fans of Eldon's. Debbie would almost always say, "I think you're acquainted with my father," and the people would reply that they were.

Eldon gradually felt better, and Debbie was obviously delighted. As they were leaving the restaurant, she said, "I see what you mean about all those autograph seekers getting to be a problem," but she was still beaming.

"Well, I guess it's just part of the whole picture for a professional athlete," Eldon said.

"I guess, in a way, you owe it to the people."

Eldon tried to look serious, but he felt stupid when he said, "That's how I try to look at it."

When they got in the car, Eldon wasn't quite sure where to go next. It was still quite early. He suggested that maybe they could take a little drive, and Debbie said that would be wonderful, that they needed time to be alone and just talk.

They hadn't gone very far before she wanted to know what had happened to make Eldon late that afternoon.

"Well, it sounds kinda dumb, but I got out a journal that my great-great-grandfather wrote. He lived here in Jackson County, back in the early days of the Church. I got all involved in it and lost track of time."

"Well, that's a nice compliment to me. You're more interested in your great-grandfather than you are in me, I guess." When he glanced over at her, she winked and pulled his hand into her lap and held it between both of hers.

"Well, it's not that, of course. I just got wrapped up in my own thoughts." Eldon was hoping she would ask what he had been thinking about, but she didn't. "There's one place where my grandfather—his name was Joseph Williams—just stops and explains how he feels about his own life. He says that his one big regret was that he didn't see sooner what really mattered in life. He says that most of what we do in this world really doesn't make that much difference."

"Eldon, that really impresses me," she said.

"Well, it is kind of interesting."

"No—I mean that you would spend your time thinking about things like that. You're anything but the so-called dumb athlete."

"I don't know, Debbie. But anyway, he said—"

"But it does impress me, Eldon. You read a lot, don't you."

"Well, quite a bit. I have a lot of time. And then it scares me that I'm going to fall behind people like you who are going to school full time."

"I doubt that. You probably learn more on your own than I do in college."

"Oh, no. What I do is too random. I still want to finish my degree when I can."

"That's really wise, Eldon. A *guy* has to do that."

Eldon had stopped for a red light. He took his hand back from Debbie so he could shift gears. "I think it's great for women to get their education too."

"Oh, so do I. But it's not the *first* thing in my life. What I want is a family. I never have felt that I absolutely *had* to finish college." She slid as close as she could in the bucket seat and took hold of his arm. Then she began to tickle his upper arm.

Eldon wanted to tell her more about the journal, but he decided to let it go for now. "I've got an idea," he said. "Why don't we stop at Baskin-Robbins and get an ice-cream cone?"

"Oh, Eldon, you *are* a growing boy. How can you even think of food after the dinner we just had?"

"I don't know." He laughed at himself. He realized he wasn't really hungry. "It just sounded fun. I don't really—"

"No, no. You go ahead. But count me out. If I ruin my waistline, you'll drop my name right out of your address book. I don't dare take the chance." She gave his arm a squeeze.

Chapter 14

On Wednesday Eldon was scheduled to pitch again, and Debbie went with him to the game. The Yankees were in town, and once again a big crowd was expected. Eldon really felt good. His shoulder felt fine, and he was confident that he could now get back to his old form.

Before the game he was sitting at his dressing stall when Les walked over to him and asked, "Did you hear about Eddie?"

"No. Is he being sent back down?"

"Yup."

"It's just because they had to make room on the roster. Tim Wolfe is coming off the injured list."

"I know. I still hate to see him go." Les leaned against the divider at the edge of Eldon's dressing stall.

"He'll be back up. He's never going to be MVP in this league, but he's solid—he'll make the team."

"I know." But Les wouldn't look Eldon in the eye.

"So what's the matter?"

"I don't know. We both knew it was him or me."

"Look, Les, when you got your chance to play for Connolly, you hit well—you earned yourself a job. That's how things work."

"I know that, Hooper. But I don't . . ." Les crouched down, looking at Eldon and speaking quietly. "I came *that* close," he said, holding his finger and thumb almost together. "I could have been the one being shipped out so easily. I got that homer in Boston, and that seemed to get me going. But it's hard to believe that my whole life could end up hinging on one time at bat."

Eldon stood up, causing Les to straighten up as well. Eldon looked straight into his face, standing close to him. "Listen, Les. There's something I've been thinking a lot about lately. If you hadn't made it at baseball, you would have done something else. The worst thing you can do is start to think that baseball is important. It's just a game we play."

"Come on, Hooper. Don't give me that. You can say that; you don't have to worry."

Eldon looked at Les for several seconds, then said, "No one stops worrying, Les. That's just the problem. But it still is a game, and if you can't have fun playing it, you're better off just getting out."

Eldon believed that, and it was a perspective that had been working its way into his consciousness for a long time. When he went to the mound that night, he tried to concentrate on it. He had been letting too many things get in the way of the joy he ought to be feeling.

And the first inning *was* fun. He got the first two batters on ground balls. His fast ball was really moving, dropping the way it was supposed to. The third batter fouled off a couple of pitches and then swung and missed. The crowd really reacted, apparently joyous to see Eldon throwing with his old form. Cheers burst sharply from close around and then came rolling down on him like grumbling thunder. Long after Eldon was back in the dugout the people were still cheering.

Jenny was in the upper deck. She had gone to the game by herself. She didn't want Eldon to know she was there, but she wanted to be where she could see him.

When the batter swung and missed, she was thrilled. She was happy to see that Eldon's arm was all right; she knew how much that would mean to him. She had made her decision now, and she didn't regret it, but she missed him. They had been close for a long time; she was accustomed to sharing in his life. Once she got back to Provo she would be busy with school, and much of the loneliness she had been feeling would be gone. But right now there was something nice about giving Eldon support—being near him—without his knowing it.

It was a good night for the Royals. The players were hitting and running aggressively, and they were playing defense as though they were protecting a no-hitter. And for a while they were. In the fourth inning Eldon gave up his first hit, but by then he had struck out three more batters, and no one had gotten good wood on the ball. He gave up another hit in the fifth and walked a man in the sixth, but when he went back to the mound in the seventh, he had a five-to-nothing lead, and his arm felt fine.

He had to face the strength of the Yankee line-up, the second, third, and fourth batters—Murphy, Winston, and Jefferson. But he felt confident he would get them. He did get Murphy and Winston easily, on a pop-up and a ground ball. That meant he could face Jefferson with two outs and no one on base. It was a good chance to challenge him, to test the shoulder. But Eldon also knew that he had to use his head.

He started out with a curve that broke in toward the left-handed batter. Jefferson was obviously guessing fast ball, for he took an off-balance swing—but a very hard one—and almost fell down as he followed through. He caught himself, then looked out at Eldon and grinned. Eldon nodded, as if to say, "Okay, now try this one." He popped in a good fast ball, at the knees. Jefferson didn't swing, and the umpire called it a ball, but it had been close. Eldon came right back with the same pitch, and this time Jefferson took his big swing and fouled the ball directly into the dirt. He nodded to Eldon again, as if to say, "Well done, but I'm not finished yet."

Eldon then wasted a pitch outside, trying to get Jefferson to chase one, but the batter let it go, and the count moved to two and two. Eldon didn't want to go to three balls—now was the time to go after him. He let go with his fast ball, really threw hard. The ball popped into Potter's mitt, and Jefferson never triggered. The umpire's arm shot into the air.

The crowd loved nothing more than to see Jefferson strike out, but they had also seen the velocity Eldon had been able to get on the ball. A lot of fans jumped to their feet. Jefferson was still standing at the plate, looking at Eldon. And as Eldon walked away, he tipped his hat to Jefferson, who nodded in return.

Eldon walked down the steps to the dugout, where the players began pounding him on the back and slapping his hands. Glen Knight told him that he was going to be tougher than ever, and Keanon came over and said, "Welcome home, Hooper."

Eldon grinned and thanked him, then sat down on the bench. He watched Debbie across the way. Her bright red blouse was easy to spot. She had brought some field glasses with her, and he could see that she had them focused on him. He looked in her direction and said, "Hi." She waved back in response.

"Oh, look at old Hooper," Becker yelled. "He's throwing kisses to that sweet young thing of his, and he's saying to himself, 'I always knew I was the best.'" He walked down toward Eldon. "Ain't that right, Hooper?"

"I guess I have to admit it, Becker," Eldon said in a

loud voice. "That's just exactly what I was thinking. But I think your way is better. You've never claimed to be the best." He paused for a couple of seconds, then added, "And you've never done anything on the field to make anyone think you're wrong."

The players liked that. They all joined in giving Becker a bad time, but Becker just laughed. And so did Eldon.

Jenny was very happy for Eldon. This was exactly what he needed. And it really was thrilling to see someone who was so good at something. She knew that she'd always been jealous of Eldon in that regard. Now it didn't seem to matter.

In the eighth inning Eldon got the first batter on a fly ball, but then he let a pitch get out over the plate, and Hoyt stroked it into right center. Oaks cut it off and held Hoyt to a single. Eldon realized that he hadn't thrown this many pitches in a long time, that he actually was feeling a little tired. But he made a good pitch to the next batter and got a ground ball. It was hit too slowly for a double play, but Reies went to second with it and cut down the lead runner. Then Pinion came up as a pinch hitter. He stayed with an outside curve ball and pushed it into right field. The runner on first went to third on the play.

Potter ran out to the mound. "You okay, Hooper?"

"I think so. There was nothing wrong with the pitch—he just went with it."

"Yeah, that's right. But you better tell the truth if you're starting to get tired. You ain't gone nine innings for a long time."

"I'm okay."

Potter trotted back to the plate. Eldon walked off the mound and wiped his face with his sleeve. It was a muggy night, with almost no wind. But Eldon was used to that, and the heat was good for his shoulder. He stepped up and threw one pitch, and was out of the inning on a routine fly ball.

When he went back to the dugout, Keanon wanted to talk to him. "Are you feeling any strain at all in that shoulder?"

"No, it feels fine, John. I've thrown some pretty good fast balls tonight, and I haven't felt a thing."

"Well, I know you have, but I probably oughta take you out. Your pitches are coming up a little, and they're starting to hit them in the air."

"I'll be fine, John. Maybe it'll be a quick inning and we'll be out of here."

"Okay. I'd like to let you finish your shutout. But they have the top of the order coming up—and they can put a lot of runs on the board when they get started. If you seem to be struggling at all, I'll be out to get you. All right?"

In the bottom of the eighth, the Royals scored two more runs, giving Eldon a seven-run cushion. In the top of the ninth he got the first two batters on a total of four pitches. There was no struggle at all. Then Winston hit a two-strike pitch right back up the middle, past Eldon's feet and into center field. That brought Jefferson up again.

Eldon liked that. He wanted to close out the game with another strike-out and leave Jefferson standing there again. He walked behind the mound and rubbed up the baseball, then wiped his face again. He had been feeling rather tired until Winston had gotten the hit, but now he felt the excitement coming back.

Jefferson was waiting outside the batter's box. He stared at Eldon with a sort of half-smile on his face. This was not for the game; it was just something between the two of them.

Eldon started him out with a fast ball on the outer part of the plate. Jefferson took it for a strike, but he had a few words to say to the umpire about it. He stepped out of the box and turned away from Eldon, his huge back and shoulder muscles flexing as he twisted and stretched. Then he stepped back in, set himself, and waited. Eldon went with a straight change-up and Jefferson swung early, fouling the ball into the crowd. He stepped out again, slammed the bat against his spikes, and then strode back to the plate, looking determined. He rolled his shoulders forward and pumped the bat back and forth.

Eldon came with another off-speed pitch, outside, and Jefferson let it go by. And again he held up when Eldon tried another fast ball in about the same place. Then Eldon came with his slider, moving inside with it, and Jefferson fouled it into the dirt.

Eldon stepped back from the rubber for a moment and took a deep breath. He didn't feel quite as strong as earlier, and he wanted this over with. When he stepped back up to the rubber, Potter signaled for a fast ball. Eldon knew Jefferson would be looking for one, but he decided to go with it anyway. He wanted to blow one past him and then walk away. He put something extra on the pitch and threw harder than he had all night. For a moment he wasn't sure what had happened—why the ball was sailing so high. But he had heard the little snap, had even felt something give way. And then, as he followed through, he felt the pain.

It wasn't a stabbing pain. Rather, it burned—like before, only much worse. He grabbed at his shoulder and stumbled forward, caught his balance, and then stood there, gripping his upper arm. There in the middle of the huge stadium, he felt the searing pain spreading down through his arm and back. No one moved; everything seemed fixed in place—a stunning silence all around him.

Eldon took one step forward, then dropped to his knees. A strange sound, like a moan, came out of the stands. It scared him. He wanted everything to be all right. And then Potter was there, saying something. But everything seemed unreal. Others were coming now—first Jefferson, and then John, and then Les. John had his arms around Eldon's waist, holding him up. "Hooper, is it the shoulder? Did it tear?"

Eldon tried to get to his feet. He just wanted everything to be okay. Cy was there now. "He shouldn't have thrown that hard," he was saying. "He was almost back."

The pain was numbing now, seeming to press down on Eldon's whole body. "It'll be all right," he finally said, but he sensed that the words were still lodged in his throat.

John helped Eldon to his feet, and he and Cy walked with him, one on each side. Les was behind them somewhere, saying, "Don't worry, Hooper. You'll be fine."

Eldon wanted to believe that. Maybe it was just like before—maybe it would just take a little time again. He tried to move his shoulder, to convince himself it wasn't so bad. But the pain rushed down his arm, stopping him and folding him forward. He held on, waited for a moment, and then took the final steps to the dugout.

In the upper deck the crowd was still standing. Jenny was perhaps the first to sit down. She put her hands over her face and gritted her teeth, but she couldn't hold back the tears. When someone asked her if she was all right, she got up and left. She wanted to go to him, but she couldn't.

She took the escalator down to the ground level and was about to leave the stadium, but she could hardly bear the thought of going home without knowing anything more. And so she went to the elevators, the place where Eldon had always had her wait for him after the games. She knew the game would be over in another few minutes. If she waited long enough, maybe she could see some of the players she knew and ask how Eldon was doing. What she really wanted was to see Eldon himself, but that would be wrong, and she knew it.

As she stood across from the elevator doors, she considered what this all meant. Maybe Eldon needed her now. Maybe it was time she forgot about herself and did something for him for once. If he knew she was with him, maybe he could get through this thing.

"Hello, Jenny."

Jenny looked up. It was Debbie Larsen. She looked stunning, but Jenny could see she had been crying. Her eyes were red, and she was holding a handkerchief in her hand. Jenny stared at her, partly because she couldn't think what to say, and partly because she was trying to adjust all the thoughts running through her head. She knew Eldon had gone out with Debbie, but somehow she'd never taken the idea seriously. Eldon and Debbie were so different. But now, as she observed Debbie's obvious concern, she saw everything in a new light.

"I just wanted to see how bad it was," Jenny said, and she realized that she was apologizing, that she felt "found out."

"I understand, Jenny. You two were friends for a long time." Something in Debbie's voice was irritating to Jenny. It was not just her speaking in the past tense; it was also a sense that Debbie was in control, that Jenny was an outsider, an intruder.

Jenny tried hard to think of something to say. "I hope it's not worse than before."

"Eldon will come back from it," Debbie said. "He does anything he sets his mind to." Jenny nodded, but she was angry. Who was Debbie to tell *her* about Eldon?

An awkward few seconds went silently by, and

then Debbie put her hand on Jenny's shoulder. "If you'd rather go home and not wait, I'll be happy to call and let you know what I find out. I know Eldon'll be glad to know you were concerned."

Jenny had been dismissed, and she knew it. But she was in no mood to fight back—not only that, she felt she had no right. Debbie was part of Eldon's life now, and Jenny was not. She twisted away from Debbie and walked away briskly. At the very least, she wanted Debbie to know that she recognized what she was up to.

And so Jenny went home. Debbie, however, didn't call, and Jenny had a great deal of trouble getting any sleep. In the morning she read in the paper that Eldon was being flown to Los Angeles again, this time for surgery. She wondered how he was taking that, what he was thinking right now. What hurt the most was knowing that Debbie was the one he had expressed those feelings to.

Chapter 15

Two days after the injury, Eldon had surgery. The rotator cuff had been torn again, much worse than before. When he got out of the hospital, he decided to go back to Kansas City. There wasn't anything to do for a while, but the thought of going back to Utah for the summer, sitting around the house with his arm in a sling, was anything but inviting. At least in Kansas City he could go to the games when the team was in town. And he could date Debbie. He needed to do that. For the past few days he had thought entirely too much about someone else.

Eldon called home and told his parents he was going back to Kansas City for now, that he wanted to stay in shape and start exercising just as soon as he could. "Eldon," his mother said, "I know what you've been telling us, but the paper here says that you might not be able to pitch again."

"I hope you don't believe everything you read in the paper, Mom."

"Now, that's what I told your dad. I said, 'If there's any way at all he can throw a baseball, he'll do it. He'd switch to left-handed before he'd just quit.'"

Eldon tried to laugh. But when his mother asked him about Jenny, he didn't know what to say. "Well,

Mom, we haven't been going out lately. And I guess we're not going to. She's decided to come back out to Provo this fall and go to law school."

"Law school! What in the world for?"

"It's just something she wants to do. Jenny always has wanted to do—you know—something interesting with her life."

"Well, it sounds sort of silly to me. You'd think the girl would know a good deal when she's got one."

"Come on, Mom. That's kind of a bad way to put it. In a way, I guess I understand how she feels."

Dad got on the phone after that. He had one of his little speeches ready. "Well, son, I'm sorry you have to go through this. But you know, you've always had things pretty much your own way. I guess now you're going to have to prove what you're made of."

Eldon said he knew that was true, but when he hung up the phone, he felt strange. He was annoyed by some of the things they had said, and yet he had recognized in them his own words coming back—just a little more strongly stated, a little less disguised.

He wanted to think more about that, to use the time on the plane to sort some things out. But the man next to him was from Kansas City, and he soon realized who Eldon was. He quizzed Eldon during most of the flight. Eldon grew increasingly tired, and by the time he got off the plane he realized he was still weak.

Debbie was waiting for him, and she looked fantastic. She smiled and waved to him, and then she stepped up and kissed him, being careful to avoid the arm that was in a sling. The kiss was somewhat warmer than Eldon expected, and he stepped back, a little embarrassed.

A man whom Eldon vaguely recognized was standing next to Debbie. "Hi, Hooper," he said. "I won't try to shake your hand." This seemed to strike the man as terribly funny, and he burst into laughter. Eldon knew him now. He was a reporter.

"Your little lady here was good enough to let me know when you were flying in. That gives me a shot at talking to you first. How did the operation go?"

"Fine, I guess." Eldon glanced at Debbie. She was smiling. Somehow he had thought she knew him better than to set him up this way.

"What did the doctor say about it?"

Eldon answered briefly and then said he ought to walk down to get his luggage.

"Ah, that stuff won't be in for a while. You know how slow they are."

"Eldon," Debbie said, "I'll go get your luggage. Is it just the one gray suitcase?"

"Yes, but it's heavy. I better go with you."

"A lot of good you'd do. Don't worry, I'll find a skycap."

This annoyed Eldon. He had carried his own bag into the airport in Los Angeles. What did she mean, "A lot of good you'd do"?

"Does this mean, then, that you are definitely out for the rest of the season?"

"I don't know. I think the doctor feels that way, but I'm not sure I do. I'll just have to see how it goes." Eldon looked around. Several people had come up close and were listening. He wanted to get away.

"Looking back on it now, do you think that John Keanon left you in the game too long? Shouldn't he have—"

"No. Listen, won't the other guys be a little upset if I give you the exclusive on all this? Maybe I ought to wait and have the team set up a press conference."

"Look, Eldon, don't worry about it. If any of them could get to you first, they'd do the same thing." He was a short man with heavy sideburns and sagging eyes. Eldon wondered how he had managed to contact Debbie. But then, he seemed the sort who would find a way. "It seems to me that Keanon never should've left you in that long. Don't you want to make some comment about that? I mean, the man might have washed up your whole career."

"Listen, my career is not washed up. And John talked to me, and I told him I *wanted* to stay in." Eldon was speaking a little too loudly, but he was starting to get angry.

"Yes, but are you the best judge in a situation like that? Of course you would want to—"

"Listen. You're not going to push me and push me until you get me to say something bad about John Keanon, and then run it as a headline tomorrow. I've been caught in that kind of trap before."

"Now, cool down, Hooper. I'm just asking. But it seems to me that what you're saying is that you do have some negative feelings about Keanon—you just don't want them in the paper."

"No! Now I'm going to say this one more time, and you put *this* in your paper. *I* chose to stay in the game. *I* threw harder than I should have. John would never do anything to hurt my career. He's one of the best men I know."

"I don't see what you're getting so defensive about, kid. It sounds almost as though you're protesting too much. It sounds to me like you—"

"Okay, this little game just ended. That's the end of the interview."

Eldon walked away. The man laughed again and called after him, "Kid, I don't know what's bugging you. I'm just asking." Eldon felt many eyes on him as he walked down the corridor through the terminal. He wanted to get out of there.

Debbie was still waiting for the baggage to come up. He didn't say much to her, and when he spotted his bag, he picked it up himself, against her protests, and marched out of the terminal with it.

"Where's the car?" he asked.

"What's wrong, Eldon?"

"Nothing." Walking fast to keep up with him, she

pointed to the car lot across the street. She looked a little confused. "Debbie, I'm sorry. I'm really tired."

"Oh, I'll bet you are." She slipped her arm around his waist and gave him a little hug. "But I'm going to get you back in a good mood. I'm taking you to a little place I know, where you can get a good meal—and it's *my* treat."

"How many reporters are you going to have waiting for me there?"

"What?"

"Nothing."

"Eldon, I couldn't help it about that guy. He knows my dad, and he knows that we've been going out. I guess Daddy told him. So he just kept calling and asking me what flight you'd be on. I didn't think you'd care that much. I didn't—"

"Never mind, Debbie. It's not that important."

In the car Eldon had little to say. He wouldn't let Debbie pay the parking fee, even though it took some effort to get out his wallet from his back pocket.

"I'm sorry, Eldon," Debbie said again as she drove out of the lot. "But I guess I don't understand why you didn't want to talk to him."

Now she was sounding a little irritated herself. Eldon shut his eyes and rested his head against the headrest. He didn't want all this. "I get tired of those guys, Debbie. He was trying to force me to say something bad about John Keanon."

"Really?"

"Yes, really."

"Well, that's strange. When he interviewed me, he was very nice."

"He interviewed you?"

"Yes. Just over the phone."

"What about?"

"Well, he knew you'd called from California. He wanted to know what you'd said and how you felt about everything. And then he asked about us, and about—"

"Us?" Eldon sat up straighter. "Was something in the paper about us?"

She looked over at him, obviously hesitant. "Well, yes. Just that we had been going out. And a little about me. Does that bother you?"

"No." He leaned back again. "Well, yes, in a way. I just think that sort of thing is my own business, and not something to put in the newspaper." But that was not what he was actually thinking. He was wondering who in Kansas City had read the story.

"You know, Eldon, you're really a very private person, aren't you."

"I don't know. I just—"

"Well, you are. I like that. For a person who has achieved so much, you're really amazing. I'll tell you what you are. You're humble. I think that's a great quality." She reached over and patted his leg, but Eldon didn't say anything. "I've missed you while you've been gone. Did you think about me at all?"

"Sure I did." But his tone had not softened. Debbie seemed to sense that she might as well leave him alone. She didn't say anything for some time as they drove along the freeway. It was getting dark, and Eldon watched the grayness set in over the fields.

"Debbie," he finally said, "I ate quite a bit on the airplane, so why don't you—"

"Oh, I didn't think of that. Well, we don't have to get anything to eat."

"I think tonight I'd better just go home and get some rest. I'm really wiped out."

"Well, okay. I understand. Maybe I could come and get you in the morning, and we could go somewhere for breakfast."

"Yeah, maybe so. If not tomorrow, we ought to do that one of these days." That was the wrong thing to say. Eldon could see Debbie stiffen. But he was not sure what to say to her right now.

When Debbie stopped the car in front of Eldon's condominium, she turned off the engine and looked over at him. "You're kind of a grouch tonight, Eldon. I think you really are tired. I'm sorry for what happened. I imagine you're worried about the future right now too. I can see how all that would make you—"

"Look, Debbie, I'm the one who should be sorry." He looked at her. She really was breathtaking. He felt sorry for her. He'd put her in a terribly awkward position. "Debbie, I *am* mixed up right now."

"Well, get some sleep. And then call me tomorrow. Okay?"

"Okay." Eldon got out of the car and met Debbie at the back, where she opened the trunk. After he got his suitcase out, he hesitated. "Debbie, actually I need some time right now. I may not call tomorrow. I might—"

"Eldon, I'm not used to . . ." She stopped. He could see that she was trying to control herself. Her breath was coming rather hard. "I'm not used to being treated this way, Eldon. If you're trying to tell me something, just say it."

Eldon set his suitcase down and looked at the ground for a time. "Debbie," he finally said, "nothing's very clear to me tonight. I'm sorry for not being . . . I mean, I'm sorry if I've been grouchy. Could you give me a couple of days to myself, and then . . ."

"Listen, Eldon, I'll give you all the time you want. But don't think I'll be sitting home waiting every moment for your call." She walked around the car quickly, got in, and drove away.

Eldon watched for a moment, then carried his bag inside and took the elevator to his apartment. It seemed dark, even after he turned the lights on. Suddenly he felt overwhelmingly alone. But this was nonsense, and he knew it. He needed to occupy himself. He thought about calling Les, but then he remembered that the team was out of town.

He picked up his bag and carried it into his bedroom, but he didn't feel like unpacking right now. He remembered that he had wanted to look at his Grandfather Williams's journal again. He wanted to get some of those ideas back into his mind. But Mac had borrowed the journal.

For one of the few times in Eldon's life, he didn't know what he was going to do in the morning. The doctor had said he would probably never pitch with the same power again, but he was not ready to accept that. For right now, however, there was nothing he could do about it. There was no way to start finding out.

Eldon wanted to look at the journal again, but, even more, he wanted to talk to Mac. Hoping that he might be in town, Eldon looked up Mac's number in his little address book and dialed it.

Chapter 16

Mac came over soon after Eldon had called. He was wearing an old T-shirt, faded green, with "Lake of the Ozarks" printed across the front. He never seemed to look any older than he had when Eldon first met him, three years before. He had Grandfather Williams's journal tucked under his arm.

"Are you feeling all right?" Mac asked as he came in.

"Sure. I'm just . . . I don't know—I'm tired, for one thing."

"What did the doctor say?"

Eldon sat down on the couch, and Mac sat down across from him. "Well, he wasn't too encouraging. My shoulder was torn pretty bad, I guess. He said if I pitch, I probably won't have much of a fast ball."

"How do you feel about that?"

Edlon was turned sideways on the couch, with his good arm hooked over the back. He looked down at the corduroy ribs of the couch fabric. "Well, I don't know. I guess I have a hard time believing it. I just feel that I'll be able to throw. I plan to do whatever it takes to build myself back up. The bad part for me is just having to sit around waiting—until I can start making some headway."

Mac laughed. "I don't know, Eldon. It sounds to me like you've got it made. You can kick back for a while, take a trip, go back to school for a while—whatever you feel like doing. You don't have to worry about money."

Eldon's problem was that nothing seemed very inviting right now, but he didn't say that. "I don't know, Mac. I've always had things I wanted to accomplish. When I try to 'kick back,' I just get nervous."

Mac nodded, affirming that he already knew this about Eldon. There was a casual quality about Mac, but he was actually more serious than almost anyone Eldon knew. And that seriousness rarely left his clear, dark eyes.

"How are your parents doing, Mac?"

"Well, Mom's not too bad. I hardly ever hear from Dad. He called me a couple of months ago, but he couldn't think of anything to say."

"Do you think he's ever gotten over your little brother's death?"

"I don't know, Eldon. He never talks about it. Neither does Mom. And they don't talk about each other. They both just seem to be going through the motions, especially Dad. It's like he doesn't care whether he lives or dies. At least Mom is dating a guy, and she seems to be doing a little better all the time."

"What do *you* live for? Why are you so different from your parents?"

Mac didn't answer immediately. Finally he said, "I don't know, Eldon. Gordy's death didn't hit me quite the same way it did them. And so much of their problem was with each other. But as much as anything, I'm left alone by their splitting up. At first I hated that, but now I'm really on my own, and I always seem to find ways to enjoy myself. You know how I am."

"But what do you want out of life?"

"Days."

"Days?"

"Yeah. I want time. So I can read and maybe see some of the world. I guess I need some money."

"You'll never have any, Mac."

"I know. That's the sad part. I'll probably find a way to see some of the world, though."

Eldon turned to face Mac. "You know, Mac, it's funny. I have exactly what *you* want. Time and money. And I've never been so scared in my life."

"What are you scared of?"

"Mostly the time. Not having anything that I really have to do. And I'm tired of being alone."

"Why don't you marry this beautiful new girl friend you were telling me about?"

Eldon would rather have avoided that topic. "Well—I don't know. I'm just not sure about that situation."

"You're still thinking about Jenny, aren't you?"

"Yes."

"You dumb jerk, Eldon. You have *everything*. Absolutely everything. And you don't even know it."

"But Mac, just because I've made a lot of money, that doesn't mean I—"

"I'm not talking about the money. You have to pay the price for your money. The Kansas City Royals *own* you. I wouldn't want to be owned."

"Well, then, what do I have? I *do* like to pitch, but I do that only about every fourth day for a couple of hours. And now I'm looking at months, Mac. Maybe I won't ever pitch again."

Eldon stood up and walked over to the window. For a few minutes he gazed out over the city, watching the lights come on in the deepening dusk. Then he sat down again on the couch and turned back to Mac. "I *know* that baseball isn't really important, but as soon as it's taken away from me, nothing else seems to matter. I've never really committed myself to anything else— not the way I have to baseball."

"And Jenny."

"Well, yes. That's true. And then look what *she* does."

"*She* does? Or did you do it?"

"Look, Mac, the problem's not just law school. She never was really committed to me, not the way I was to her."

Mac stretched his legs out in front of him, sliding down in the chair. He was much smaller than Eldon, but he had a way of commanding his share of the space. "Okay, Eldon. Do you want to hear my little two-bit analysis of you?"

Eldon laughed, wanting to keep this fairly light, but Mac still looked serious. "Okay. Analyze me."

"Baseball used to be way too important to you—or let's say *winning* was. I do think you've brought that more into perspective. But that's not the heart of the problem. The thing is, Eldon, you've never found anything inside *yourself*. You can't always be looking outside for your pleasure in life. No one else will ever give you what you are looking for—not even Jenny—and baseball is temporary, even if you play for quite a while yet."

"Mac, no offense—that's a good analysis—but I already know that. I've known it for quite a while. One of the reasons I've been trying to read and think more lately is that I want to develop myself into something more than I've been. But I don't seem to be getting anywhere."

"Then why don't you go to the source?"

"What do you mean?"

"Now, that's really ironical, Eldon. *You* are asking *me* that? You're the guy who tried to convince me that I ought to pray."

Now Mac had struck too close. Eldon had thought about this, too. He just didn't like to face it. He leaned back and tried not to show his reaction, but he didn't say anything.

"Last year some guys from your church—missionaries—set up a little booth on campus. So I stopped by and talked to them, mainly because of what you'd told me. They gave me a bunch of brochures and asked me if they could come and talk to me. So I said okay, and they came a few times. They were nice guys, and we had some good talks. But they kept trying to give me 'lessons,' and I kept getting them all mixed up by throwing out all kinds of questions. I guess they just finally gave up on me."

Eldon laughed. "I thought you were going to say you had converted."

"Well, who knows? It's not impossible. But Eldon, you're my prime example of a Mormon. And frankly, you disappoint me a little. I see in your theology—and I especially find it in your grandfather's journal—a power and security that's supposed to come from God. It's supposed to fill you with a sense of purpose and faith. But—"

"Mac, wait a minute. I know what you're talking about. I think I've come a long way from what I was a couple of years ago."

"Well, okay. That's probably true. But religion still seems to be a sort of backup for you. It's something that helps, but I don't think it's the core of what you are."

Eldon nodded. "Mac, remember that it took my Grandfather Williams a long time. Even at the end of his life he was very disappointed with himself."

Mac sat up straight. "I know, Eldon. That's a good point. But I guess I especially watch you because you're about the only person I know who's trying. I want to see you do it. Maybe I could be convinced if I could see someone actually *demonstrate* that there's something to this whole business."

Eldon leaned back and shut his eyes. He really was very tired. "Mac, do you ever feel that so much of what you are has been passed along to you? That you were made into something before you had the chance to decide whether that was what you wanted to be?"

"That's part of the whole problem, Eldon. It's easy for me to sit back and watch you—and take a few shots at you, for the fun of it. But taking what you are and changing yourself into something more is, well, I don't know. Maybe it's impossible. It's a sort of miracle when someone does it."

"I guess you have to go to the source again."

"If there is one, Eldon. I'm not sure I even believe that."

"Do you ever pray any more?"

"As a matter of fact, I do. Quite often. But I can't say that it's helped me any. I've been trying to move mountains. I keep praying that some of those good ski slopes out in Utah will move out to Missouri. But they won't budge."

"You better pray for some different mountains, Mac. God wants those Utah mountains to stay right where they are."

"Yeah, well, I don't think they're in any danger. Not with me doing the praying."

"I don't know, Mac. You take your praying more seriously than some people who claim to be believers."

"That's true, actually. But I can't seem to tap into any of that power that I keep reading about. That's why I want you to do it, Eldon. You're my one hope."

After Mac left, Eldon sat in the dimly lighted living room and thought over everything Mac had said. He felt better in a way. He seemed to have a diagnosis now, something to come to grips with. And yet, only one clear idea came to mind—one first step that he wanted to take. He got up and walked into his bedroom and called Jenny.

Chapter 17

Jenny was surprised. She hadn't expected Eldon to call, and for the moment she wasn't sure how to react. She felt pleased, even excited; the truth was, she'd been hoping he'd call since the day he'd first driven away. All the same, another side of her kept saying that this would only get her all mixed up again.

She asked Eldon about the surgery and about his plans. He told her about the operation, then said, "Jenny, do you think we could get together and talk?"

"Do you mean tonight?"

"No. Maybe tomorrow."

"I'm working, Eldon. I won't be home tomorrow."

"What about tomorrow evening?"

"Well, okay. But Eldon, I'm not sure . . ."

"Look, Jenny, I'm not sure either. But after going together so long, I think it was stupid to break up the way we did. I acted like a little kid."

Jenny held her breath for a moment. "Eldon, I've missed you. I would like to see you. But . . . I mean, you're going with Debbie Larsen now, aren't you?" Jenny knew she was fishing; she had been terribly jealous since the night at the stadium.

"Yes, we've been going out. And maybe something will work out there. But Jenny, I just keep thinking about you, and I'd like us to talk things over in a more sensible way at least once before we let the whole thing go."

Jenny hardly knew how to understand her emotions. On the one hand, she had wanted Eldon to say he was finished with Debbie, and yet, at the same time, she was scared. "Well, all right," she said. "I'd like that too. But Eldon, I haven't changed my mind about law school. I'm definitely going."

"Okay."

There was a long silence. "What time should I expect you?"

"Early, if that's all right. Say, six-thirty?"

"Seven might be better."

"All right. Let's just go somewhere where we can talk."

"Okay, but Eldon, let's not . . . well, never mind." Jenny didn't know what she wanted to say. Then she surprised herself by saying, "I can't tell you how good it is to hear your voice."

When Jenny hung up the phone, she felt very strange. She didn't want to allow herself to get excited about this. She had no idea how anything could be worked out between them. And yet she was happier than she'd been in weeks, and her whole family noticed it.

Jenny had a luncheon date the next day with a woman she'd met in the law office where she worked. The woman, Camille Stone, was a lawyer—and a Mormon—which interested Jenny very much. She spent the morning thinking about Eldon more than she really wanted to, so when Mrs. Stone came by for her, she was happy for the chance to talk to someone.

On the way to the cafeteria, Mrs. Stone said, "Do me a favor, Jenny, and call me Camille. I need to feel young, even if I don't look it." But Jenny thought she looked very good. She was probably around sixty, a pretty woman with graying hair and strikingly white teeth. She was a careful dresser, her clothing neat and tailored, and she was an exacting speaker; yet, there was a pleasant ease about her.

They went through the cafeteria line together and then found a table. "How long have you been practicing law, Camille?" Jenny asked.

Camille spread her napkin on her lap. "Well, it's hard to say. I've done it in fits and starts. I didn't go to law school until my older children were teenagers—or I guess Alice was only about ten. Then Johnny came along, much to our surprise, when I was forty-one, so I took some years off and stayed home with him. Then a couple of times I've gotten overwhelmed by trying to do everything, and I've taken some rather long leaves of absence. Fortunately, the firm has always let me come back."

"Hasn't it been hard for you—I mean, with a family and all?"

"Yes, it has. Sometimes. And I've felt guilty about it at times too." She took a sip of water. "Johnny got hurt at school once, and I was in court. No one could reach me. When I got to the hospital that afternoon, I felt like a pretty lousy mother. His dad had been with him through the whole thing."

"Well, that was good."

"I guess so. But I was furious. The truth of the matter is, I was jealous. Sometimes I've watched the kids go to their dad for things I wanted to give them—and that's not been easy for me. But I guess it *is* good in some ways. They certainly love that man."

"Is he actually home more than you are?"

"No, but he's more flexible. He has a business, but he's never been married to it the way some people are. When he feels he has to leave, he lets his help take over. He used to run the kids to piano lessons, and he'd knock off early so he could see them in track meets or baseball games—whatever was going on at the time. I missed out on a lot of that sort of thing."

Jenny was thinking. She had never really pictured these kinds of situations. It was a new perspective.

"Jenny, from the nature of your questions, I suspect you're wondering whether you really ought to go to law school."

"No, I've made up my mind. But I . . . well, I guess I think only about school and not much about life afterwards."

"Well, now, that's exactly how it started with me. I first went to law school—I don't know—for the challenge of it, I guess. Not many women were doing that twenty-five years ago. But I'd been home for fifteen years, and I was starting to have some real troubles, especially with depression. My kids were needing me less and less, and I had no idea who I was. So Glen said, 'Why don't you go back to school?'"

"Your husband wanted you to go?"

"No, not at all. I think it's the last thing he wanted. But he could see what was happening to me. I was going to pieces."

"Did some people think you were doing the wrong thing?"

Camille finished her salad before answering. "Oh, listen, there were women in my ward who implied— not very indirectly—that I was a fallen woman. In fact, the only one who seemed to really understand was my bishop. He said, 'Camille, you have to lead your own life. I think, in your case, going back to school might be a very good thing.'"

Jenny still had lots of other questions she wanted to ask, but she hated to seem too nosy.

"Jenny," Camille said, as if reading Jenny's mind, "are you getting pressure—from certain quarters—not to go?"

"Not exactly. My parents think I'm crazy, but they aren't really pressuring me. I was going with a guy—

and I guess most people think I'm stupid not to get married."

"Is that the baseball player?"

"How'd you know that?"

"Well, I think your boss mentioned it. It seems to be your greatest claim to fame."

"I know, Camille. And I'm sick of that. That's exactly what I was heading for—being nothing more then Eldon Haller's wife."

Camille laughed. "Well, this is good to find out. You're young, but at least you're not as smart as I thought you were. Now you don't seem nearly so threatening."

"What's that supposed to mean?" Jenny was staring at Camille, but she was smiling.

"Well, I don't know much, Jenny, but I've learned a couple of things. And one of them is not to live your life by the measure of what other people think. Whether people think you're only a baseball player's wife doesn't really matter, not even slightly. What matters is what the baseball player thinks, and what you think."

"Okay," Jenny said. "I agree with that. Although I *do* get tired of the way people identify me almost completely by my friendship with Eldon. But I think what scares me is that I'*d* always feel that way about myself. I'd feel like I'd never really done anything with my life."

"Yes. You're dumb, all right. Who would have guessed it?" Camille took a bite of food and chewed slowly, watching Jenny. Jenny smiled again, but she didn't say anything. "Jenny, do you really think law school is 'doing something with your life' any more than anything else is? If you want a law degree so that people will think you're important, you're making a big mistake. You are who you are, and what you happen to *do* for work really doesn't matter very much."

"Then why did you go to law school?"

"I told you. I was going crazy."

"But why not elementary education, or driver's training, or P.E., or—"

"Well, I thought I had aptitude for law. And then— I thought it would make me sound important." She waited for Jenny to look up, and then she smiled. "Well, I used to be dumb too."

"I'm glad to hear it."

"Look, Jenny, I'm just saying that I really can't stand people who think that once they have a professional degree, they have some automatic right to respect. What I see you doing is competing with your baseball player, saying, 'If you're someone important, well then, I'll be someone important too.' You probably know better than anyone else that baseball has nothing to do with that boy's worth—if he has any."

"It's made him a millionaire."

"Which is one of the things you hold against him, right?"

"I don't know. I don't think so." Jenny was starting to feel a bit over her head in this conversation. Camille seemed to be coming at her from all sides at once.

"Of course you do. The poor guy can't help it that he's rich, you know. It's all those crazy people in the world who made him that way. The question is, is he anything besides a baseball player?"

"Yes, he is," Jenny said, seriously. And then she laughed. "He's very cute, for one thing."

"Oh, I know. I saw him when he spoke in church one day. He gave a pretty decent talk, too. He sounded to me as though he'd thought about a few things in his life."

"He *does* think."

"Well, I'll tell you one thing, Jenny. I wouldn't play down that 'cute' business too much. When you wake up in the morning, it's not bad at all to look over at someone cute next to you. And I like a man with shoulders. Your baseball player really has a set of shoulders on him."

"Camille, you're . . . one of a kind."

"That's part of getting old. Now I can say all these surprising little things and sound rather wise. But I don't underrate what you're facing. If I were you, though, I'd get my own answers and then I'd live my own life. I wouldn't spend a lot of time wondering what everyone else was thinking, and I wouldn't do a lot of second-guessing myself."

"I'm not, Camille. I'm going to law school."

"And what about Hooper what's-his-name?"

"He doesn't want me to go."

"Well, then, I think that's your answer. He sounds like the domineering type. You could never live with that."

"No, actually he's not domineering at all. In fact, he would pay to send me to law school. What I mean is, he doesn't want me to go back to BYU this fall. He wants to get married now."

"And you don't want to take his money. Right?"

"Well, no, it's not that. I just—"

"Jenny, do you like this guy?"

"Yes, I do."

"I don't get this. It sounds as though you're running away to win some kind of symbolic victory."

Jenny took her napkin from her lap and put it on the table, even though her food was only half eaten. "I don't think so, Camille. I can see why you might come to that conclusion. I've even thought about it that way myself. But the main thing is that I don't want to get married and then have to drop out of school because of a family, and end up never reaching my goal. I want to find out how good my mind is. I want a challenge. If I don't do it, I'm afraid I'll always feel cheated."

"Will he wait for you?"

"No. I don't think so."

"Jenny, look at me. I'm now going to say something full of the wisdom of age. This tired old face will help you to know how wise I am." Jenny laughed, and Camille smiled, but she seemed rather serious. "Life is short. That is something you don't know. At your age it seems long. But it is not. Just remember that when you are trying to make a decision."

Jenny nodded, though she was not really sure she saw the implication in what Camille was saying.

"If the baseball player won't negotiate—if he won't wait, or work things out—maybe he's not worth it. But if you love him, and you're playing games, I'd say you're making a big mistake. Very soon now you're going to be old, like me, and then you'll know that you don't have time to be dumb. But the fact is, you don't have time now. It's important to do the right thing."

Jenny was staring at Camille, still trying to grasp what she was saying.

Camille set her napkin on the table, never taking her eyes off Jenny. "Wrong decisions last just as long as right ones, Jenny. You know better than anyone else whether you're playing games. And you know how to get the right answer. You know where to go to get it."

Chapter 18

Eldon waited until afternoon before he finally forced himself to call Debbie. But he knew it was something he had to do.

"Debbie, I called to apologize," he said. "I'm sorry for the way I handled things last night."

"I'm sure you were tired."

"Well, yes, I was tired, but there were some other things going on too. You know, I've had a lot to think about."

Debbie seemed to respond to that. "I know, Eldon. I should have been more patient. I'm sure the injury is a big worry to you."

"Actually, it's not that so much. I mean, I am worried about it, but I'm also trying to work out some other things." Eldon had been standing in the living room, but now he sat down on the couch. "Maybe you won't want me to tell you this, but it just seemed to me that I should."

"Tell me what?"

"I'm going to see Jenny Davis tonight." There was no response. "See, the thing is, when we broke up it was mainly because she wanted to keep going to school. In a way, I guess I wanted—"

"Eldon, you don't have to explain this to me." Her voice sounded suddenly aloof.

"I know I don't, Debbie. But I thought I should. The point is, she and I broke up because I wanted to get married. While I was out in Los Angeles I started to realize that was a strange reason." He hesitated, but she didn't respond. "I just need to talk to her one more time. I guess I just want to be sure we did the right thing. After all, we did go together for a long time." He wished that Debbie would say something. "To tell you the truth, I don't think anything will come of this. I don't think anything has changed. She's still planning to go to law school this fall. But, anyway, I just thought it was fair that I should tell you I was going to see her."

"Eldon, you don't need to account to me for anything. If you think I'll be home crying tonight, you can forget it. I have a date myself. So if it's sympathy you're handing out, save yourself the trouble."

"No, that's not at all what I had in mind. I thought we were—you know—interested in each other. I'd still like to keep going out and—"

"*If* Jenny Davis is not available. I'm sorry, Eldon, but I'm not accustomed to being second choice."

"I didn't mean it that way, Debbie."

"I don't think you know what you mean, Mr. Haller. You need to get your act together. You need to learn a few things besides how to throw a baseball—especially since you may not have an arm to throw with anymore."

Nothing was said for a moment, and then for some reason Eldon started to laugh. "You're probably right about that," he said. This seemed to leave Debbie baffled. She mumbled something that Eldon couldn't understand. "Well, anyway, Debbie, it's probably good we had this nice little chat. I think we've had a little trouble really getting to know each other, but now I have a feeling we understand each other pretty well."

Eldon was getting ready to say good-bye and hang up when Debbie said, "Eldon, I didn't mean that . . . about your arm. I really do hope it gets better."

"Well, thanks. I hope things go well for you too."

When Eldon hung up the phone, he wasn't angry. In fact, he felt sorry for Debbie, and he didn't blame her for being upset. She had a point. He *did* need to get his act together.

When Eldon picked up Jenny that evening, the Davises were friendly, but everyone seemed nervous and self-conscious. Sister Davis gave him a little hug and told him how happy she was to see him. This was strange, in a way, since she saw him every week in church, but he was in their house again, and she was obviously putting a lot of hope in that.

Bishop Davis also seemed a little too obvious, smiling and shaking Eldon's left hand, trying too hard to seem natural. He'd just asked Eldon about his arm when Billy came rushing in and jumped up against Eldon, practically knocking him over. Sister Davis warned him to be careful, but Billy paid no attention. "Eldon, where've you been?" he said. "Jenny's been home for a long time."

Eldon bent down and put his arm around Billy's shoulders. "Hey, how're you doing? Have you been playing any baseball?"

"Sure. But I need you to help me. Why don't you come over anymore?"

Eldon was struggling to think of something to say when Rosemary came to his rescue. "How's your shoulder feeling?" she asked. She had grown up a great deal in the last year, had become very pretty.

"Not bad," Eldon said, straightening up. "I'm just supposed to be careful with it for a while."

"Will you miss the whole season now?"

"At least. The doctor's not really sure I can pitch at all after this."

"But you will," Bishop Davis said.

"Eldon," Billy was saying—in fact, he had been

saying it over and over for quite some time—"let's go play now. I'll get my glove."

"But I can't, Billy. Look at this thing on my arm."

"You can throw with the other one."

"You sound like my dad."

At that point Jenny finally came down, and she managed to get Eldon out the door, although Billy followed them all the way to the car. Jenny wondered whether she should drive, but Eldon said he could manage all right. When they were finally backing out of the driveway, she said, "What is this charm you have over my family?"

Eldon couldn't think of anything to say. He suddenly felt very strange, being alone with her again. She seemed relaxed, however. She was wearing a soft blue dress, the color of her eyes. Eldon hadn't seen it before, and he hoped she'd bought it for tonight.

"It's nice to see you, Eldon," Jenny said. "You look awfully good for a guy who just had surgery."

"I've missed you," he said. He wanted to say a lot of other things, but he didn't. He was not going to rush in this time and make a fool of himself again. "I thought maybe we could just go down to that pizza place where we always used to go. Is that all right?"

"Why don't you take *me* to Carlton's?"

"What?"

"Come on, now. Don't you think I know what you've been up to?"

"If you want to, Jenny, we could . . . how did you hear about that?"

"Things get around, Eldon. My mom has a way of finding out everything."

"Jenny, if you want to go to a nice place, that would be fine with me. I just wanted—"

"No. That's fine. Actually, what I really want to do is something *fun*. Why don't we go to Worlds of Fun?"

"The amusement park?"

"Right."

"Are you kidding?"

"No. Come on. Let's do it."

"You're wearing a dress."

"Take me back. I'll change."

Eldon shook his head. "I don't know about you, Jenny," he said. "Look, I want to talk. If we go out there, we'll—"

"We can talk later. We have all evening."

"You'll never change, you know that, Jenny?" But he was smiling.

"Will you take me?"

"No."

"Why not?"

"Because I couldn't do anything. Those rides would pull my arm right off. All I could do is stand around."

"Okay, what else could we do?"

"I don't know. Maybe a movie. But I really don't—"

"All right. But something really stupid. Why don't you pull in at that grocery store up ahead and I'll get a paper."

Eldon pulled over, and Jenny got a newspaper. An old Woody Allen movie was playing at a mall not too far away. Eldon protested that he would draw too big a crowd in a mall, but he drove there all the same. The theater had an outside entrance and there was not much of a line, but they had to wait for about ten minutes.

"You're going to like this movie, Eldon," Jenny said. "It'll raise your spirits."

Eldon couldn't believe he was doing this; he was starting to let Jenny's mood influence him. It really was nice just to be with her again. But behind him, in the line, he could hear people whispering his name, and others walked by and then stopped to stare. He tried to talk to Jenny and not notice them.

For a moment it seemed that people were going to leave him alone, but then Jenny said, "Don't look now, but that lady over there has found some paper in her purse. I think you're about to come under siege."

"Would you mind knocking her down and sitting on her?"

"Forget it. She's twice as big as I am."

It was too late. The woman—a large one in very crowded shorts—was upon him, with a line of kids trailing behind her. "Excuse me," she said, "aren't you Eldon Haller?"

"No, ma'am," Eldon said.

"Oh, excuse me. I'm sorry. I—"

"It's all right. I must look like him. Once before someone asked me the same thing."

The woman nodded, and blotches of red appeared along her neck and cheeks. She mumbled another apology and was gone.

Eldon stood perfectly still for several seconds, and then he looked down at Jenny. Her mouth was wide open. "I don't believe you did that," she said.

Eldon grinned, looking very satisfied with himself. Jenny began to laugh, not hard at first, but she couldn't seem to stop. After a time she put her head against Eldon's arm, and he could sense she was trying to stop, but now she was shaking all over. When she looked up again, there were tears in her eyes. "Eldon, I still can't believe you did that. You're always so . . ." She was laughing too hard to continue talking.

"I've been wanting to do that for a long time," he said. "But it's your fault. You bring out the worst in me." Eldon was whispering, obviously concerned that others would hear them.

"But you did it so innocently. I didn't think you even knew how to lie."

Eldon smiled again. Just then someone tapped him on the shoulder. "Say, Hooper, would you mind signing this for me?" A teenage boy stood there with a slip of paper in one hand and a pen in the other.

For a moment Eldon just looked at him; then he

said, "I can't write worth a darn with my left hand. It wouldn't look like anything at all."

"That's okay," the boy said. "I'd know what it said." Two more kids had stepped up next to him, also holding scraps of paper. The people in the line in front of him had turned around as well. Suddenly he was in the middle of a little crowd, and others were approaching.

"I'll tell you what," Eldon said. "Catch me when my arm is better. If this thing doesn't heal, you won't want my autograph anyway."

"No, come on," the boy was saying, and suddenly Eldon took Jenny by the arm and began steering her quickly toward the car.

"I'm sorry," he said as he opened the car door for her. He went around to the driver's side and got in. It was hot in the car, but he didn't start the engine immediately. "Jenny, I know that was stupid, but—"

"I don't blame you," she said.

"Sometimes I just want to be able to go anywhere I choose and not be watched all the time."

"It's okay. Let's just go get some pizza."

"Let's buy one and take it back to my place."

"Okay—but not a frozen one."

"Right," he said smiling. He started the car and flipped on the air conditioner. "Jenny, what was all this about anyway? Did you really want to go to Worlds of Fun?"

"Yes."

"Why?"

"Because I wanted to be *with* you for a while. I wanted to have fun, the way we did during other summers. I'm afraid that once we start talking, we'll find we're right back where we were the last time we tried."

Eldon looked back toward the theater entrance. "Those people are probably all saying what a jerk I am."

123

"I doubt it. They probably feel bad that they ran you off."

"Do you love me, Jenny?"

"Yes."

Eldon continued to look straight ahead for some time, and then he looked over at Jenny. He tried not to smile, but he couldn't help it. "Do you want my autograph?" he said.

Chapter 19

They stopped and picked up a pizza and then drove to Eldon's place. When Jenny walked in the apartment, she took a good look around. "Do you know that I've never been here since I helped you move in?"

"I guess I ought to get a few pictures or something for the walls. I'm not very good at that kind of thing."

"You need my touch, Eldon."

"I know." Eldon set the pizza on the kitchen table and got a container of milk out of the refrigerator.

As they ate, they talked, mostly small talk. Jenny told him about her job, and Eldon told her about Mac and about Les, and they talked a little more about Eldon's injury and the rehabilitation program he would be starting as soon as he'd healed enough.

"Eldon," Jenny said, "on the night you reinjured your shoulder, I was at the game. Did you know that?"

Eldon was surprised. "No, I didn't," he said, "but then, there wouldn't be any way I could have known. Where were you sitting?"

"In the upper deck." Jenny decided not to say anything about Debbie or what had happened after the game. But she had satisfied a suspicion.

"No wonder I didn't see you," he said, adding, after a moment, "but I'm glad you were there. It sounds like you just couldn't get over me." He smiled.

"Unfortunately, I'm afraid that's right," she said, and she smiled too.

This was certainly the opening Eldon wanted, but he still knew he had to be careful, to move slowly. "Jenny, I couldn't get over you either. So where do we go from there? How do you feel about things now?"

Jenny took a drink of milk, then set the glass down slowly. When she finally looked at Eldon she said, "Well, I feel quite different tonight from the way I did yesterday at this time, but I'm still awfully mixed up."

"What do you mean?"

"I had a long talk at lunch today with a new friend—a woman named Camille Stone. She's a lawyer. And then I went home and talked with Mom for a little while. And after that I went to my room and did some praying. I'm starting to see that I've been very selfish—that I've only thought about myself in all this. And I'd like to work something out." For several seconds she looked down at the table again, and then she said, still not looking at Eldon, "But I still want to go to law school. I really think it's what I *should* do. It's developing the abilities I have, and that's very important to me, Eldon."

"I have no problem with that, Jenny. We can work it out so you can go."

"But you say that so easily, and I'm not sure it *is* easy. It's too late to get into school out here, and I hate to lose that time. And you know how it scares me that if we get married I'll end up having to quit—because of a family. But listen to me, Eldon. You can see how selfish I still am."

Eldon slid his chair back a little and stretched his legs out. He supported his injured arm with his other hand. "I don't know that you're being so selfish, Jenny. It's right to want to grow." He sat for a time and tried to clarify his thoughts to himself before he spoke again. "Jenny," he finally said, "I had a long talk with Mac last night. He forced me to think about some

things that I don't like to deal with. I've been thinking
about them all day. I know that I've still got a lot of
growing up to do. I need more depth, more spiritual
direction. I need more faith."

"Eldon, you're so far ahead of most of the guys I
know. You have so much—"

"Don't say that, Jenny. Mac's right. I claim that the
Church is the center of my life, but the truth is, the center is still baseball. I've got to do something about
that."

"That's a problem for everyone. Look how much
value I'm putting on law school."

"Okay, that's right, maybe. But that's the point I'm
trying to make. If we're going to work this thing out
between us, the first thing we have to establish is what
really counts. Then I think the rest will fall into place."

"What does count the most?"

"Well, that's one of the things I've been thinking
about today. I think we start by committing ourselves
to each other and to certain purposes. It's fine to say
that religion comes first, but what does that mean
exactly? I think we have to decide what specific things
we are committed to—the things that can't be com-
promised."

"Have you decided what those are?"

Eldon sat up straight again and leaned toward
Jenny, placing his elbows on the table. "Well, yes, in
one sense. They're all the things we've been taught all
our lives. But that doesn't mean much until you apply
it to your own life and get down to particulars. I want
to talk about our commitment to each other first."

"Eldon, the very word scares me. I immediately
start thinking about what I'm going to have to give up.
I know I shouldn't feel that way, but—"

"It's okay, Jenny. Some of the things you're scared
of just don't exist. You think you'll lose some sense of
self if you marry me, because I'm a baseball player. But
think about it, Jenny. I'm probably in more danger

than you are. You're too strong-willed to be robbed of what you are. Now, isn't that true?"

She nodded. "Is that an argument that I don't need to go to law school?"

"No. I want you to go. I think it's something you need to do. But we can work that out. Right now we need to promise ourselves to each other."

"But Eldon, it isn't that easy. What do you mean, 'We can work it out'?"

"Look, Jenny, everything's up in the air right now. Maybe I'll never play baseball again. If I don't, maybe I'll go on a mission while you're going to law school. But I think I *will* play. It's what I think I'm supposed to do. I have a feeling that the Lord wants me to use *my* gifts. But we could wait for a while, if that's what is best. Or I could go to BYU this fall, while you go to law school, and get in a semester while this arm is coming around. And if it doesn't, I may need a good lawyer to sue somebody. I don't know, Jenny. I just think we can work things out so neither of us will feel cheated."

"It's not just us, though. What about children?"

"I know. I've thought a lot about that. There's no question that kids have first priority. We can't compromise on that. But I don't think we have to. The thing is, Jenny, a life has seasons. I think you'd want to be home if we had small children, but that wouldn't be forever."

"Which brings us right back to the original question. How can I have all the things I want? I just get sick of going around that circle whenever I think about all this."

"But that's what I just said, Jenny. A life has seasons. You wouldn't always have—"

"But there's still that period of time when I would have to sacrifice all my goals—or at least put them on hold. It's not that I don't think I ought to. I just don't feel ready. I don't think I'm mature enough, Eldon."

It was not a time to push, and Eldon knew it. There

were things that she had to settle for herself. He got up. "Let's go sit in the living room," he said, reaching out for her hand.

She walked with him into the living room, but when he sat on the couch, she wandered over to the bookcase. She glanced at the books for a moment and then said, "Mom says it really isn't that much of a sacrifice, or that she never thinks of it that way, but I'm not very much like my mother." Eldon didn't say anything. Jenny was still looking at the books. "Eldon," she asked, "where did you get these?"

"What do you mean?"

"Aren't they mine?"

"No."

"But about half of these are books I read in college."

"I know."

Jenny turned around and looked at Eldon. "But why?"

"I don't know. I just always asked you what you were reading, and then I tried to get hold of whatever it was. If I couldn't find it here, I could always find it in Boston or New York."

"I can't believe it. You have almost everything— even stuff I sold back to the bookstore. Have you actually read it all?"

"Most of it."

"Why didn't you ever tell me?"

Eldon didn't know why, exactly. And he found that he was embarrassed now. He couldn't bring himself to look at her directly. "I'm not sure, Jenny. I guess it seemed too much like some stupid do-it-yourself education program. And then sometimes I wasn't even sure I had understood what I had read. Some of those things—Shakespeare and Milton and—"

"You read Milton? What, *Paradise Lost?*"

"Let's just say I *tried* to read *Paradise Lost*."

"Eldon, that's incredible. But I still don't understand. Why did you do it?"

"Well . . ." Eldon let his breath out slowly. "I guess I wanted to know what you were thinking about."

She was looking at him strangely—intently. "Thinking about?"

"Jenny, I didn't want to seem like some dumb jock to you. It seemed that if I knew what you were thinking about, I'd understand you better, and we'd gradually *be* more alike." He continued to look down for a time. When he did look up, he saw tears on Jenny's cheeks.

"Eldon," she said, "I can't think of anything that anyone has ever done for me that is more . . . unselfish. You're so . . ." Her voice caught and she couldn't finish.

"Jenny, it wasn't that big a thing. Part of it was just fear. I didn't want you to get too far ahead of me."

"Eldon, if I spent my whole life running at top speed, I could never keep up with you. You have such a clear sense of what needs to be done, and then you do it. All I do is wander around looking at doors I want to open; most of the time I can't even reach the doorknobs."

Eldon motioned for her to sit down beside him. As she leaned her head against his chest, he reached out and put his arm around her. "All day," she began, but she couldn't control her voice. In a moment she started again. "All day I've been praying I would get an answer tonight." But she didn't say anything more—or couldn't.

"Will you marry me, Jenny?"

"Yes."

"When?"

"I don't know. Don't make me think right now. We have a ton of things to figure out, but right now I just want to keep feeling this way."

For some time they just sat there. Eldon was having some trouble controlling his own emotions, and he didn't dare try his voice. Finally Jenny said, "I think we're supposed to kiss now, aren't we?"

Eldon thought that sounded right.

Chapter 20

The dugout was amazingly quiet. The players were talking among themselves, but they were doing very little yelling, the way they normally did. Of course, Eldon knew why, and it struck him as rather amusing. He turned to Les, who was sitting on the bench next to him. "Do these guys really think I'm not aware I have a no-hitter going?"

Les laughed. "You said it—I didn't."

"Do you believe that stuff about jinxing a guy if you mention a no-hitter?"

"I don't know. But I'm not going to be the one to do it."

Eldon grinned. "Well, I'll tell you the real trick, all right?"

"Okay."

"You say to yourself, 'I have three outs to get. If I get 'em, that means I just pitched my first-ever no-hitter in the major leagues.' And then you say to yourself, 'And what if I don't get those three outs? What happens?' And you answer, 'Nothing at all.' And then you go out and get the three outs just because you might as well, since you're pitching anyway."

"Are you serious? Can you really do that?"

"Well, not entirely. But that's the secret."

"But you want the no-hitter, don't you?"

"It would be nice," Eldon said.

"You'll get it, Eldon."

"Thanks, Les. I hope so."

Tim Wolfe had just grounded out, and that meant it was time to go back out on the mound. Eldon saw Eddie get up from the bench and walk down to John Keanon. John was apparently putting him in at shortstop, because of his strong defensive abilities. Eldon was glad about that, but he knew Eddie would be nervous. "Hey, Eddie," Eldon yelled, "if you let one go through your legs, you owe me a root beer."

"Don't worry. I might dive on one, but ain't nothing going through my legs."

Eldon smiled. "It's just a game, Eddie."

Eldon wished Becker hadn't been traded the winter before. Becker could have said the wrong thing and helped everyone relax.

When Eldon walked out of the dugout, the crowd responded, but with a certain nervousness. There was very little yelling. Perhaps they too didn't want to jinx him by mentioning the no-hitter. However, he took his warm-up pitches with a sense of comfort and confidence. He knew when he was in command. No one had come close to getting a hit off him, and he had nine strikeouts. He had walked a batter in the second inning, and that had been the only base runner for California. Eldon's fast ball was not quite what it had been before the injury, but no one in the major leagues had better command of his pitches or a better sense of how to keep batters off stride.

Eldon stood straight, waited for the first batter to step in. It was Billy Douglas, who was an aggressive batter, a free swinger. Eldon thought Douglas would probably attack the ball, probably go after the first pitch. Potter signaled for a slider and set the target outside and low. Eldon hit the target perfectly, keeping the ball just off the outer edge. Douglas chased it and rolled it off the end of his bat toward the second-base side. Eldon tried to get to it but couldn't, so he hurried on to cover first. He took the throw from the first base-man—a close play.

The crowd burst into a tumult, obviously relieved, but then the nervous quiet set back in as the next batter stepped to the plate. Eldon used his fast ball, inside, to keep the batter back a little, and then he came with his big curve. The batter popped it up. Glen Knight was a little more animated than usual in getting under it, but he caught it—and Eddie was right with him, backing him up.

Now the crowd was really going crazy. They seemed not to be able to contain themselves anymore. Eldon glanced over at John Keanon. He seemed stiff as a board. Eldon grinned. If nothing else, he wanted to get this last out for John.

It would have been interesting to have Roger Jefferson coming up now, since he now played for the Angels, but big Earl Wells was almost as good. As Eldon looked in for the sign, the crowd quieted suddenly. This out seemed terribly important to them.

Potter wanted to start with a fast ball again, but Eldon shook the sign off and went with his curve. He didn't think Wells would be guessing curve ball on the first pitch, and he was right. Wells swung early and awkwardly, almost falling down. The crowd screamed with delight.

Now Eldon came inside with a fast ball, but Wells laid off it. So Eldon tried the fast ball a little outside. Wells took a big cut and fouled the ball off. There was a quick burst of pleasure in the crowd, and then the tension settled over the stadium like a fog. For some reason, it was hard for Eldon not to laugh. It seemed to mean so much to everyone. He hoped Mac was listening, or was even at the game. He would understand better than anyone there—except for Jenny—what it really meant.

He wasted another pitch inside, and then he got the sign he wanted—curve ball. Wells may well have been looking for it now, but Eldon didn't believe he could hit it, not the way the thing was breaking tonight. "I thank Thee," Eldon whispered. "I don't deserve so much."

He felt the breaths draw in, and then he fired, letting the ball snap over his fingers. He could see the spin on the ball, and he watched it break, hard and down. Wells swung and missed.

Suddenly everyone went crazy. The players were jumping on him from all directions. John Keanon was there, screaming, "You did it, Hooper. You did it." The guy was actually crying.

Eldon staggered ahead, trying to get loose from his ecstatic teammates. His eyes searched the box seats. He didn't realize Jenny had come down and was just above the Royals' dugout. Then he saw her waving. She wasn't jumping up and down, not the way most of the crowd were, but then, she was five months pregnant. She looked so beautiful!

He pulled loose and ran toward her, leaping up onto the top of the dugout. She was nodding, smiling—crying—but she couldn't seem to say anything. Eldon reached over the fence and hugged what he could reach of her.

She said something but he couldn't understand. "What did you say, Jenny?"

"No one else knows what it took, Eldon."

He nodded, and now he felt tears in his own eyes. "From you too," he said.

A man with a microphone had climbed up next to Eldon. "Congratulations," he yelled, slamming Eldon on the back.

Eldon was still looking at Jenny. The broadcaster stepped almost between them and thrust the mike at Jenny. "You must be very proud, Mrs. Haller."

"Yes, I am."

"Her name is Jenny," Eldon said.

"Excuse me, Hooper. What did you say?"

"I said her name is Jenny—*Jenny* Haller."

"Oh, yes."

"She just finished her second year of law school."

"Is that right?" The man seemed a little confused. "Well, Eldon, you must be very proud."

"I am. Believe me." He looked at Jenny. "She's right at the top of her class. She's a brilliant woman."

"Is that right? But what I meant was—"

"And did you know we're going to have a baby this fall?"

"Eldon, you knothead," Jenny said, "he means about the game." But Jenny Haller was still crying, big tears running down her cheeks.